# Christian Liberty Nature Reader

## Book Five

# Christian Liberty Nature Reader

# Book Five

Written by
Worthington Hooker, M.D.

Revised and Edited by
Michael J. McHugh

*Christian Liberty Press*
Arlington Heights, Illinois

Originally published as *The Child's Book of Nature*
Copyright © 1890 by Harper & Brothers

Copyright © 1992, 2002 Christian Liberty Press
*2017 Printing*

General editorship by Michael J. McHugh
Revised and edited by Michael J. McHugh and David K. Arwine
Copyediting by Christopher Kou
Cover design by Eric D. Bristley
Layout and graphics by Christopher and Timothy Kou at
**imagineering studios, inc.**

A publication of
*Christian Liberty Press*
502 West Euclid Avenue
Arlington Heights, IL 60004
**www.christianlibertypress.com**

ISBN 978-1-930092-55-6
     1-930092-55-5

Set in Berkeley
Printed in The United States of America

*The original version of this book was written by Dr. Worthington Hooker in the late nineteenth century. In the year 2002, the editors of Christian Liberty Press significantly revised and modified the original text to bring it into a greater conformity to the Word of God and true science.*

# TABLE OF CONTENTS

# Preface

This particular textbook is designed not only to improve a student's reading skills and comprehension, but also to increase the student's understanding of and interest in God's wonderful creation.

The Bible says we are to do "all for the glory of God" (I Corinthians 10:31). Reading for God's glory necessitates reading material that draws attention to Him and His truth, that reflects His majesty, and that meets the standards of Holy Scripture. What this means is that we should compare any reading selection to the standard in Philippians 4:8 and ask these simple questions: "Is it true? Is it noble? Is it right? Is it pure? Is it lovely? Is it admirable? Is it excellent? Is it praiseworthy?"

The *Christian Liberty Nature Reader* Series seeks to follow these standards set forth in the Scriptures. Believing that the student can gain an enhanced appreciation for God by studying His creation, (Psalm 19:1; Romans 1:20), this textbook seeks to present the majestic splendor of His handiwork, seen in both the animal and the human realm.

It is our prayer that this series will give to the reader the joy that is to be associated with "good reading," and that the knowledge imparted will help "make wise the simple" (Psalm 19:7)

Michael J. McHugh
*General Editor*

THOU OPENEST THINE HAND, AND SATISFIEST THE DESIRE OF EVERY LIVING THING

Psalm.cxlv. 16

# Chapter One

# *How Food is Used*

## What Is Made from Blood?

In this chapter, you will learn why your body needs blood to develop and operate properly. As you learn more and more about how your body works, remember to praise the wonderful Creator whose wisdom designed each and every function of the human body. Everything in a plant or tree is made from the sap. This is, then, the building material, as we may say, of the plant. In much the same way, everything in your body is made from blood. The blood, then, is to your body what sap is to a plant. It is the common building material of the body.

As an example, consider a rose. It is made from the sap that comes to the bud through the vessels in the stem. In the same way, the little finger of the child becomes the large finger of the man, from the blood that comes to it through the vessels in the arm. As the stem of the plant grows larger in time, so does the arm of a child. The sap makes the stem grow, and the blood makes the arm grow.

If you cut off a branch of a plant, it stops growing because the sap no longer comes to it. It soon dies and decays. If the arm of a child is cut off, it cannot grow, because no more blood can come to it. Like a branch that has been cut off, it dies and decays.

A twig comes up out of the ground. It grows larger and larger every year. Soon it is a small tree. After many years it becomes very large, and spreads out its long branches over a great space. As you look up at it, think of all that you see, its branches and leaves, as having been made from the sap that is continually running in its pipes. As the little twig becomes a tree, so the infant in the cradle becomes a large man. When you look up at a man, think of his whole body as having been made from the blood that runs everywhere in its vessels, just as you think of a tree as being made from the sap.

As you continue to read, you will see that many of the plants and creatures that God has created are similar in structure or function. You will learn more about this in Chapter Seven.

How different from each other are some of the things that are made from blood! For example, you may find it hard to believe that hard, white teeth are made from the same blood that the soft, red gums are. Suppose that while you are in a chinaware factory a man should tell you that even the whitest china is made from a red liquid, and that in this factory they also make fine cloth from this liquid. You might not believe him. But white chinaware and the fine red cloth are not very different from your teeth and the gums.

Suppose, now, that he should show you a yellow, bitter fluid, and then a clear, soft water, and tell you that he makes these from the same red liquid from which the china and the red cloth are made. This, certainly, would be difficult to believe. And yet, in our bodies, bile and tears are made from the same blood as teeth and gums.

Not only are a few diverse things made from blood, but many things that are very unlike each other. Suppose that the chinaware maker should tell you that besides making white china and red cloth from his red liquid, he made also a variety of both hard and soft things, such as velvet, various kinds of cloth, nails, and glass. Impossible! you might say. But this is no more wonderful than that hair, teeth, gums, nails, bones, and all the different parts of the body should be made from that same red fluid — blood.

The body is the house or habitation of the soul. It is a well built and a well furnished house. The bones are its timbers. The skin is its covering. The hair is its thatched roof. The eyes are its windows. It is a house that can be easily moved about, just as the soul wishes. There is a great deal of machinery in it. Our body has little cords, called nerves, running to all parts of this machinery, like telephone wires. There are also other kinds of machinery, such as the breathing machinery, the machinery for taking care of food, and the machinery for circulating blood. The brain sends out messages everywhere by the little cords, and receives messages by them. Through your brain, you think and act, and sometimes sleep. This part of the house is very curiously and beautifully fitted.

As you have read, all the various parts of this house are made from the blood, and yet there is more variety in them than there is in the materials that man uses to build houses. Suppose that a man should show you a large quantity of a red liquid, and tell you that with that he intended

to build a house and furnish it — that he would make from it all the stones, bricks, timbers, glass, nails, plaster, carpets, mirrors, chairs, and curtains. You would say that the man was absurd. But God makes from the blood all the parts of the house of the soul.

Exactly in what way all the different parts of the body are made from the blood, we do not know. Wise men have studied this a great deal, and they have found out some things about it. Nevertheless, with all their wisdom, they do not know enough to make skin, hair, or anything else that you see in your body from blood any more than they can make even a simple leaf from sap.

# Review

1. From what is everything in a plant made?
2. From what is everything in your body made?

3. How is the plant bud like your finger?
4. How is the plant's stem like your arm?
5. What kinds of things are made with blood?
6. Of what is the body said to be the habitation?

# How is Blood Made?

You have learned what is made from blood, and now you will want to know how the blood itself is made.

The blood in your body is made from the food that you eat. It is made very much in the same way that the sap in the plant is made. This may sound strange to you, but it is true. The plant's food is in the ground, and the root is like its stomach. The roots absorb the plant's food from the ground. In much the same way, your stomach absorbs the nutrients in the food that you eat.

The roots do not absorb all of the soil, but only absorb what is needed to make the plant grow. The stomach of an animal or human doesn't absorb all the food either; it absorbs only that part of the food that can be used — the part that will make good blood. There is no sap in the ground, but there is material that can be made into sap. So there is no blood in your food, but food has material that can be made into blood. It is the job of the root to take in material that will make sap, and so it is the job of the stomach to absorb material that will make blood. They generally work very faithfully. It is very seldom that they take in what they ought not to.

You have seen how many different things are made from

blood. This is very wonderful. But it is also wonderful that blood can be made from the many different kinds of food that you eat. Just think of all the various things that you eat at dinner — meat, potatoes, turnip, squash, applesauce, cranberry, celery, pie, raisins, and many others. It seems strange that red blood can be made from such a mixture as this. But it is so. There is something in all these different things that helps to make blood.

Blood is made from different things in different animals. The cow, of course, never eats meat. It would be of no use in its stomach. The cow's stomach would not be able to absorb anything from meat, for God has designed its stomach to absorb materials from grass, meal, and grains, but not from meat. The Creator has made the stomach of the cow in such a way that it can get from grass what is needed to make blood. And He has given such a stomach to a dog that blood can be made from the meat that it eats. Thus, grass would be of no use to a dog. Our stomachs are made in such a way that our blood can be made from a great many different things; so the variety of our food is much greater than that of animals such as the cow and the dog.

# Review

1. From what is blood made?

2. How is an animal's stomach like the root of a plant?

3. What part of the food do the roots of plants and the stomachs of animals absorb?

4. What is the difference between the food that a cow eats and the food that a dog eats?

5. How are our stomachs different from those of the cow and the dog?

---

# The Dust of the Earth

The food of plants is in the ground, and the roots take it up. The food of animals is in the ground as well. And yet, if we should fill our stomachs full of earth, we would not be nourished. Why is this? It is because the food is not in the right form for us while it is in the earth. It must be changed before our stomachs can do anything with it.

This is what the plants do for us. They get this food out of the earth for us, and put it into a form that our stomachs can use. We eat bread made from wheat. It nourishes us and blood is made from it. But what is wheat? It is grain that is made from the sap that comes up through the vessels of the stalk, and this sap is made from the material that the root sucks up out of the ground. You see, then, that what the wheat is made from is in the ground. All the plant does is take this up out of the ground and make it into wheat, so that our stomachs can use it for food. The plant's root, then, we may say, gathers food out of the ground for our stomachs.

One of the things that we eat is sugar. Where does it come from? It is made from the earth, air, and sunlight. But even if you could put earth, air, and sunlight into your stomach, no sugar would be made from them in your body. There are plants that do this for us. They make sugar for us to eat from the earth, air, and sunlight.

The same thing is true when you eat meat. This meat was once a part of the ground. See how this is. Suppose it is a piece of beef from an ox. The grass that the ox ate was made from the earth, air, and sunlight; from this grass, blood was made in the ox; from this blood the meat was made. From the meat, blood is made to nourish you.

See how many changes the food in the ground goes through before it becomes a part of your body. First it becomes sap, then it becomes a part of the grass, then in the stomach of the ox it is sucked up, and is changed into blood; then it becomes a part of the ox, then it is sucked up in your stomach, and is changed into blood. Now it is ready to be used in your body to make nerves, bones, eyes, teeth, or any other part of the house of your soul.

You sometimes drink the milk of the cow. This also comes from the earth, air, and sunlight. The cow goes to the pasture and eats the grass that is made from the earth, air, and sunlight. The cow's blood is made from the grass, then milk is made from the blood, and this milk is changed back to blood in your body.

So you see that all our food really comes from the earth. There is in the earth under our feet just what makes and nourishes our bodies. We cannot get at it ourselves, mixed up as it is with the earth, but the plants suck it up and prepare it for us.

You can also see from what you have learned in this chapter the meaning of the Bible verse, "Dust thou art, and unto dust shalt thou return." (Genesis 3:19) We are dust, or earth, for we are made from it and are nourished by what comes from it. When we die our physical bodies will become a part of the earth again, while our souls will live on eternally.

You see that there are two reasons why animals and human beings have stomachs to put their food in. One reason is that they want to move around. An animal could not have a root for a stomach, as a plant does. An animal must have a stomach that it can carry around with it. We can imagine an animal made like a plant. It might have feet with roots sprouted out from them, and these roots might have little mouths that would suck up food as soon as they were put into the ground. But how very awkward and inconvenient this would be! The animal would be obliged every now and then to bury up its feet with their roots in loose, moist earth, and stay still in one spot until enough was sucked up from the earth for its nourishment. And, the roots would be dangling around and catching in everything as the animal moved. In the same way, your feet could not carry you around as nimbly as they now do if you had roots fastened to them. Another reason is that the food in the ground is not fitted to nourish humans or animals. It must be gathered up in plants and be changed in them, as I have shown you in this chapter, before it can be of any use to animals or human beings.

The roots of a plant are much larger than the stomach of an animal. The stomach of an animal is but a small part of its body, while the root of the plant is nearly as large as the plant itself. What do you think the reason for this is? The root of the plant absorbs only a small part of the earth, the plant's food, and so it takes a great deal of earth to give the plant all the sap that it needs. It is for this reason that the root spreads out so far on every side. In the animal the stomach absorbs a great part of the food. It does not require a large stomach, for it needs only a small amount of food. You see, then, that the food of the plant is bulky, as we say, and therefore it must have a large root, while human beings and the animals can manage food with a smaller stomach.

## Review

1. From where do animals get their food?

2. What must animals do in order to use their food?

3. How are plants useful to us?

4. What is wheat? How do we use it?

5. Where does sugar come from?

6. Explain the text, "Dust thou art, and unto dust shalt thou return."

7. Name two reasons that an animal needs a stomach.

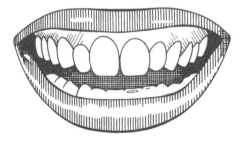

# Chapter Two
# *Important Tools for Eating*

## The Stomach and Teeth

The stomach, as I have told you, absorbs from the food that which is made into blood, but it does not do this as soon as the food is put into the stomach. The food must be digested first. You may have heard about digestion, and now you will learn what it is.

When you swallow your food, there is a liquid in the stomach that mixes with it. This liquid slowly breaks down all the different kinds of food until it is all one great lump. The meat, potato, and pie, are not only well mixed, but they are so changed that you could not tell one from the other.

When the food is broken down in this way, the stomach begins to work on it. It absorbs a white fluid very much like milk, and it is from this fluid that all the blood in our bodies is made.

Now observe what is done to the food before it goes into the stomach. There is a mill in your mouth for grinding it up, and a very good mill it is. There are many teeth there for the purpose of grinding up your food very finely. You can see what the use of this is. The finer the food is, the more easily the digesting fluid in the stomach will change it. It takes some time for this fluid to soak through a solid piece of meat or potato. So you see that you must not swallow your food too fast, but must let the mill in your mouth grind it up thoroughly.

Sometimes people help the plants by grinding up the minerals and food in the soil. In the spring the gardener digs up his garden, and the farmer ploughs his fields. What is this for? It is to loosen up the ground, and to break up the ground for the plants, so that they can draw more food out of it. If this were not done, the hard earth would be to the plants just as your food would be to your stomach if you swallowed it without chewing it well. Your teeth do to your food what the spade and the plough do to the food of plants.

While the mill is grinding the food, there are some factories inside the mouth, making and pouring out a fluid to moisten it. This fluid, called the saliva, is what you feel in the mouth when your mouth waters. The two largest of these factories are just below your ears. These saliva factories do a moderate business generally. Most of the time they only make enough liquid to keep the mouth moist. Sometimes they do not make enough even for this. This is the case when your mouth gets dry, as it does when you have a fever. When you eat, these factories do a quick job, for they then have to make a good deal of fluid to mix with the food. It may seem as if they know when it is necessary for them to go to work and make more saliva than usual. This, of course, is not so; but how it is that they are made to work so hard while we are eating, we do not know.

The food of plants, or soil, needs moistening just as our food does. The rain moistens it for the root, the stomach of the plant, so that it may get nourishment from it. When you water the dry earth in a flowerpot, you do for the food of the plant what the saliva factories do for your food.

As I have just told you, sometimes, in fever, the mouth is very dry. This is partly because the saliva factories have almost stopped working; hardly any saliva comes through their canals into the mouth. It would be hard work to eat dry food then. A dry cracker must be moistened before it can be eaten. This is very much like what sometimes happens to plants when there has been no rain for a long time. There they are, with their roots in the ground, just as they have been all along. The food is close, but it is so dry that they cannot manage it. They languish and wilt. The dry earth is to them like the dry cracker to the fevered mouth.

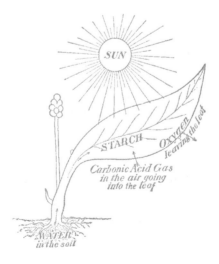

# Review

1. What does the stomach do to the food?

2. What does the stomach absorb?

3. What happens to the food before it goes into the stomach?

4. Why is it important to grind the food?

5. What else is done to the food as the teeth are grinding it?

6. Describe the work of saliva factories.

7. Why must the plant's food be moistened as well?

# More About Teeth

Inside of your mouth there are different kinds of teeth. They are for different purposes. The front teeth are for cutting the food; the large back teeth are for grinding it up finely; the pointed teeth, called the canine teeth, are for tearing the food.

You can see these different kinds of teeth in humans and animals. Every animal has such teeth, as each animal needs to divide its food. The dog and the cat eat meat, and they must tear it to pieces to eat it; they therefore have long, sharp, tearing teeth; so, too, have the lion and the tiger, for the same reason. Now look at the cow's mouth; it has no tearing teeth. The grass that it eats does not need to be torn; it needs to be ground up. For this purpose the cow has large, broad, grinding teeth. These are its back teeth.

But you notice that the cow has a few different teeth in front; they are made to cut. Now watch a cow as it eats grass, and see how it uses these two kinds of teeth. With the front teeth it bites the grass and cuts it; then with the end of its tongue it pulls the grass back where the grinding teeth are, to be ground before it goes into the stomach. So the cow has in its mouth both a cutting machine and a mill. The horse also has these two kinds of teeth, as you see represented in this figure, which shows the skull of a horse.

When you eat an apple you do very much as the cow or the horse does with the grass. With your front cutting teeth you bite off a piece; then it is pushed back where the grinders are, and the grinders crush it into a soft pulp before you swallow it.

The cow does not always use its cutting teeth in the way that I have mentioned. Watch the cow as it eats hay; it does not cut this as it does the grass. With its front cutting teeth, the cow merely takes up the hay, and the hay is gradually drawn back into the cow's mouth, the grinders all the while working on it. If the hay is in a rack, the cow pulls it out with its cutting teeth. It is the same with the horse.

That beautiful and unique animal, the giraffe, also has these two kinds of teeth. This animal, when fully grown, is three times the height of a tall man; it eats the leaves of trees, which it crops with its front teeth, grinding them up with its large back teeth, as the cow and horse do

with their hay and grass.

Notice that your tearing teeth are not nearly as long and powerful as those of dogs, cats, bears, etc. Why is this? It is because although you eat meat as they do, you can, with your knife and fork, cut up your food. They do not know how to use such things, and so God has given them long, sharp teeth to tear their food to pieces.

The cow grinds the grass and hay twice. So do sheep, deer, camels, giraffes, and many other animals. The cow eating grass in the pasture grinds it partly in its mouth as it crops it, and then stows it away in a very large stomach that it has for the purpose of storage. After a while the cow stops eating, and you see it standing or lying in the cool shade chewing its cud. That large stomach is very full of grass now, and this all needs to be chewed over again. How do you think this is done?

After the grass is well soaked in this large stomach it passes into another, for the cow has more than one stomach. It has four. In the second stomach the grass is all rolled into cud balls. This is a very curious operation. Each one of these balls goes up into the mouth to be chewed again. After it is well chewed, down it goes again, but it goes into still another stomach, and then up comes another ball to take its place; and so the cow goes on until all the cud balls are chewed. If you look at the cow's neck while it is doing this, you can see when the ball goes up and when it goes down. The cow seems to have the same quiet enjoyment while chewing its cud that the cat has when, with its eyes half open, it lies purring and lashing its tail after a full meal.

Birds have no teeth. A bird's mill for grinding food is not in its mouth, it is in its stomach. This mill is called the gizzard. A hen picks up the corn that you throw to it. It swallows it very fast. Where do you think it goes? It goes into a bag called the crop. Here it is soaked, just as the grass is in the large stomach of the cow. When it becomes soft enough it goes into the gizzard. It is then crushed by little stones that the bird has swallowed, making a soft pulp, as corn is ground in a mill between two millstones. If you cut open the gizzard of a fowl, you can see the stones that the hen has swallowed to grind up the corn. They do it quite as well as teeth would. Birds that live on softer food that does not need grinding do not have gizzards, but have common stomachs.

## Review

1. Name the different kinds of teeth in your mouth. What are they for?

2. How are the teeth of dogs and cats different from yours?

3. Describe the teeth of the cow.

4. Describe how a cow chews its cud.

5. What is the crop of a bird for?

6. What is the gizzard for?  Do all birds have gizzards?

# Chapter Three
# *Important Systems for Life*

## The Circulation of Blood

Many young people do not know how sap circulates in a plant. It goes up through one set of pipes, and goes down through another set. It is the same with the blood in your body; it is always in motion. There are two different sets of pipes for it to go back and forth, as there are in the plant for the sap. These two sets of pipes are called arteries and veins.

The blood in your body is kept in motion by a pump that works all the time, night and day. This pump is in your chest. It is the heart. Put your ear to someone's chest, and you can hear it working as it pumps out the blood. You can hear it in your own chest sometimes when it works very hard. When you have been running very fast you can hear your heart beat.

The heart pumps blood out at every beat into the large artery. From this great main pipe other arteries branch out everywhere, and from these branches other branches go out; dividing in this way, like the branches of a tree, the arteries at last are very small and narrow.

At the ends of the arteries there are exceedingly small branches, called vessels. The smallest ones are called capillaries, from the Latin word *capilla*, which means a hair. They are really smaller than the finest hairs, for you cannot see them. When you cut your finger, you split a great many of these vessels, and the blood oozes out from them. When anyone blushes, these capillaries in the skin of the face become very full of blood, and this causes the redness. It is the blood in these little vessels that makes the lips pink. These capillaries run throughout your body, so that wherever you prick yourself with a pin the blood will ooze out.

The blood is pumped from the heart by one set of pipes, and comes back to the heart by another set. It goes out from the heart by the arteries, and it comes back to the heart by the veins.

Some of the veins lie very deep, and some lie just beneath the skin. You can see some of them under the skin in your arm and hand. But you cannot see the arteries. Nearly all of them lie deep beneath the skin. Think of the reason why God has designed it this way. If an artery of any size is wounded, it is difficult to stop its bleeding, because the heart is continuously pumping blood through it. But it is easy to stop the bleeding of a wounded vein because the blood is traveling slowly back to the heart. Because it is so dangerous to wound arteries, God has placed them deep in the body so they cannot easily be wounded.

The Maker of our bodies has guarded the arteries in another way as well. He has made them much stronger than the veins. If they were not made very strong they might burst now and then. You sometimes see the hose of a fire engine burst when they are working the engine very hard, but though your heart sometimes pumps very fast and hard, as when you have been running, not one of the arteries gives way. But they would burst if they were not made stronger than the veins.

The blood in the arteries is red, but the blood that comes back to the heart in the veins is dark. This is the reason that the veins that you see under the skin look dark. You will learn more about the dark and the red blood in the next section.

You see that the blood is kept in motion in a different way from the sap in trees. In a large tree there is a great deal of sap running up in its trunk, but there are no large pipes there like our arteries and veins. The sap goes up and down in a multitude of very small pipes. There is no pump in the tree, as there is in our bodies, and in the bodies of the animals.

The heart is at work all the time, while you are asleep as well as when you are awake. If it should stop pumping blood, you would die. How steadily it works, going thump-thump all the while! How much work it does in a lifetime! It takes but a few days for it to beat a million times.

Suppose you were to count up how many times it beats before the days of twelve years were finished. You would be surprised at how much your heart worked. After twelve years your heart beats almost half a billion times.

It would be well if we, whether children or adults, would

take a lesson from this little busy worker in your bosom. If one goes right on performing cheerfully every duty as it comes along, he will do a great deal in a lifetime, and he will do it easily and pleasantly if he does not keep looking ahead and thinking how much he has to do.

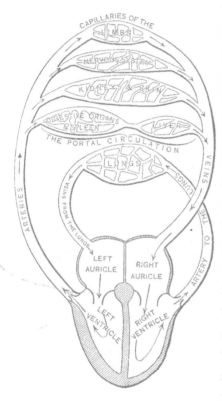

There is a pretty story, by Miss Jane Taylor, about a discontented pendulum. The pendulum of a clock in a farmer's kitchen, in thinking over the ticking that it had to do, became discouraged, and decided to stop. The hands on the clock face did not like this, and had a talk with the pendulum about it. The pendulum was, after a while, persuaded to begin working again because it saw, as the hands said, that it always had a moment to perform every tick in. The pendulum's foolish waste of time in complaining made the farmer's clock an hour too slow in the morning.

# Review

1. How is the circulation of blood similar to the circulation of sap?

2. Describe how the heart works.

3. Describe the arteries and capillaries.

4. How does the blood come back to the heart?

5. How are arteries different from veins?

6. How is the color of the blood in the arteries different from the blood in the veins?

---

# Breathing

Why do you breathe? That is plain enough, you say. You cannot live without breathing. But why is it that your life depends on your breathing?

You remember that the blood coming back to the heart through the veins is dark. It has been used, while it was in the capillaries, for building and repairing the bones, skin, muscles and nerves. It is not fit to be used again as long as it is dark. What shall be done with it? It must be made in some way into good red blood again. This is done in the lungs.

Just as fast as the dark blood comes to the heart, it is sent to the lungs to be made into red blood, and then it goes back to the heart to be sent throughout the body. But how is the dark blood changed into good red blood in the lungs? The air that you breathe in does it. Every time that you draw a breath, air fills the lungs and the oxygen in it changes the blood that is found there.

And now you see why it is that you have to breathe to keep alive. If the air does not go into the lungs, the dark blood that is there is not changed into red blood; it goes back to the heart as dark blood, and is sent all over the body. But this dark blood cannot keep you alive. It is the red blood that does this. You see, then, how death is caused in drowning. The air is shut out by the water, the blood is not changed in the lungs, and the heart stops beating. Then, of course, the person or creature dies.

The heart and the lungs fill the space in your chest. The lungs cover up the heart, except a little part of it on the left side. This is where you can feel its beating so plainly. Here is a figure of the heart and lungs. The lungs are

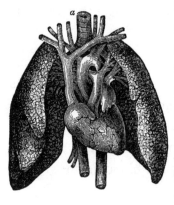

spaced apart, so that you can see the heart and its large arteries and veins. You see the windpipe, marked **a**, by which the air goes into the lungs. The lungs are light and spongy. They are light because they are full of little cells for the air to go into. It is in these cells that the blood is changed by the air.

What about fish? How can they live without air? You may say that fishes do not breathe, and it cannot be that they have lungs, for they would be of no use to them. It is true that they do not have such lungs as we have; but they have gills, and they really do breathe. How is this, you will ask, when they live in the water? There is a good deal of air always mixed up with water, and the gills of a fish are so designed that the air in the water can change the blood in them. The gills of a fish are like its lungs, and the way that they are used is interesting. The fish takes water into its mouth, and lets it run out through the gills, and so the air that is mixed with the water changes the blood in them. The gills of fish are thin, and the arteries and veins in them are very thin tubes. The air in the water easily goes through the thin tubes, and the blood is aired by it, as it is in the lungs of land animals. But, the air that the fishes breathe is mixed with water. Our lungs are fitted to breathe air alone, but the fish may be said to breathe air and water together. Air alone does the fish no good. It must have air mixed with the water, or it is of no use to the fish.

Here is a picture of the lamprey. You see that it has a row of holes on its neck; these are openings that lead to  its lungs. There are seven holes on each side. It is from this that it is sometimes called seven-eyes. Insects have such openings into their lungs. The grasshopper has twenty-four of them, in four rows. So you see that different animals have different ways of breathing. They do not all breathe through their mouths and noses, as we do.

You see that the chief purpose of breathing is to air the blood, but it is of use to us in another way as well. It enables us to speak. We could not speak if we did not breathe. The sound of the voice is made at the top of the neck, in what we sometimes call the "Adam's apple." This is a sort of musical box at the top of the windpipe. In this box there are two flat cords stretching right across it. This is called the voice box. It is marked **a** in the diagram. When we speak or sing, the sound is made in this way: the air rushing up out of the lungs strikes the cords, and makes them vibrate or shake. It is just as the vibration of the fiddle string makes a sound when the bow is drawn over it. If you look at an Aeolian harp fixed in a window, you can see that the strings are made to quiver by the wind, and this causes a sound. In the same way, the air that rushes up from your lungs makes the cords in the Adam's apple vibrate, and the chest may be said to

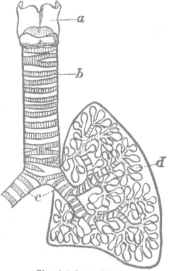

The air tubes and lungs.

*a* larynx or voice box.
*b* trachea or windpipe.
*c* bronchi.
*d* air sacs

be the bellows of that little musical box or organ that you have in the throat.

Many animals have a voice box in their throat similar to ours. The lowing of the cow, the barking of the dog, and the mewing and squalling of the cat are all done in such a box. You perhaps have wondered how the cat purrs. This noise is made in the same box where it does its mewing and squalling. If you put your finger on a cat's throat while it is quietly purring, you can feel a quivering motion there.

Fish have no voice. They have no voice box. If they had they could not use it, for the only way in which it can be used is to blow air through it. The frog cannot use its voice box while it is under water. It has to stick its head up out of water when it wants to croak.

# Review

1. Why must you breathe?

2. How is the blood changed in the lungs? What would happen if the blood was not changed?

3. Where in the body are your heart and lungs?

4. How do fish breathe?

5. What other purpose does breathing have besides changing blood?

6. Describe how your voice works.

7. How does it work in animals like the cat and-frog?

# The Brain and Nerves

You have learned some things in the previous chapters about how the body is built and kept in repair. You have learned that the blood is the building material from which all the parts of the body are made. Food, you have seen, is used to make the blood, and the purpose of breathing is to keep the blood in good order. The heart, with its arteries and veins, keeps the blood moving all about the body, so that it may be used in building and repairing.

Let us now see how you use the machinery of your body. Raise your hand. What makes it move? It is what we call the muscles. They pull your arm and raise it. But what makes them do it? They do it because your brain tells them to do it. It is your thinking brain, then, that makes the muscles raise the arm.

But the brain is not there among the muscles. It is in your head. How does the brain get at the muscles to make them work? It does not go out of the head to them, as a man might go out of his house among his workmen to tell them what to do. The brain stays in the head all the time, but there are white cords, called nerves, which go from the brain to all parts of the body, and the brain sends messages by these to the muscles. The muscles do what the brain tells them to do.

These nerves act like the electrical wires of a building. The head is the brain's "office," as we may call it, and here the brain sends out messages by the nerves as electricity is sent from a power station by its wires. When you move your arm, a message goes from the brain along the nerves to the muscles, and makes them act, but how that message works we do not know.

If the wires that go out from an electrical power station are broken off in any way, the electrical impulse in the wire may send out signals, but they will not go to the places they are supposed to reach. The electrical signal would not flow along the wire, stopping instead where the break is. In the same way, if the nerves that go to the muscles of your arm are cut, the muscles cannot receive any message from the brain. You might think very hard about raising your arm, but the message that your brain sends to the muscles is stopped where the nerves are cut, just as the electricity stops where the break is in the wire.

While the brain sends out messages by one set of nerves, it receives messages by another set. It receives them in the form of the senses. If you put your finger on anything, how does the brain in your head know how it feels? How does it know whether it is hard or soft, rough or smooth? The brain does not go from the head down into the finger to find this out. It knows it by the nerve cords that stretch from the brain to the finger. When you touch anything, a message is sent, as quick as a flash, from the finger along these nerves to the head where the brain is, and lets it know what kind of a thing it is that your finger has touched. So when you smell anything, it is the nerves that connect your nose with the brain that tells you what kind of a smell it is. And when you taste anything, it is the nerves in the mouth that tell the brain whether it is bitter, sweet, or sour. When you see anything, it is the nerve that connects the eye with the brain that tells you what it is that you see.

The brain is the softest part of the body. You can get an idea about what your own brain looks like by looking at the brain of some animal at the meat market. You can see it very well in a calf's head when it is prepared for cooking. We have compared the nerves to the wires that stretch out from the electrical station. But there are relatively few wires in an electrical station, while the nerves that branch out from the brain, all over your body, are too

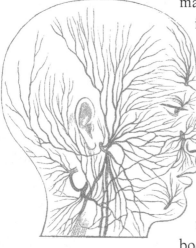

many to be counted. Here is a figure showing how the nerves branch out over the face and head. There are a great many of them, and so there are in all other parts of the body.

The nerves branch out so that there are little nerves throughout the body. If you prick yourself with a pin anywhere, there is a little nerve there that connects that spot with the brain, and that tells you that it hurts. All the nerves in all parts of the body have their beginnings in the brain. In this soft organ are bundled together, as we may say, all the ends of the nerves, so that the brain can use them. There the brain is at its post, constantly learning through the nerves what is going on in all parts of the body.

How great a job the brain has in attending to all these

signals from the ends of nerves! And how amazing it is that the brain does not get confused, when it receives so many messages through the nerves from every part of the body! It always knows where a message comes from. It never mistakes a message from a finger for one from a toe, or even a message from one finger for one from another.

And so, too, in sending out messages to the muscles, there is no confusion. When you want to move a finger, your brain sends messages by the nerves to the muscles. It does not go sometimes to the muscles of another finger by mistake. You always move the finger that you wish to move. And so with all other parts. Messages go from your busy brain to any part that you move. You can see how wonderful this is, if you watch anyone who is dancing or playing on an instrument, and think how the messages are all the time going by the nerves so quickly from the brain to the different parts of the body. You will learn more about this in another chapter.

The brain receives messages from the senses by one set of nerves and sends messages to the muscles by another set. If you burn your finger, you pull it away from the fire. Now, in this case, the brain gets a message from the finger by the nerves, and so knows of the pain. The message goes from the finger along the nerves to their ends in the nerve center in the brain, which receives it. What does the brain do? Does it leave the finger to burn? No, it sends a message at once along some other nerves to the muscles that can pull the finger out of harm's way.

# Review

1. Describe what happens when you raise your arm.

2. How does the brain tell the muscles what to do?

3. Describe the nerves.

4. How does the brain receive messages?

5. How does your body react when you burn your finger?

# Chapter Four
# *The Senses*

## Seeing

The senses by which the brain obtains most of its information are the sight and the hearing. In this section we will look at the organ or instrument of sight.

The eye is a very beautiful instrument. It is very wonderfully made, and it has a great many different parts.

What we call the white of the eye is a strong, firm sort of ball. It is filled mostly with a jelly-like substance. It is this that makes it a firm ball. If it were empty it would be like a bag. At the front of the eyeball is fitted a clear window called the lens. The light goes in through the lens. Light cannot get in through the sides of the eyeball, through the thick white of the eye.

Through the lens you can look into the ball of the eye. You cannot look through the jelly-like substance that is there, and see the very back of the inside of the eyeball. It is like looking into a dark chamber. The reason that it is so dark is that it is lined with something almost black. If this were not so, the eyes would be dazzled with the light that goes into them, just as they now are when the light is very bright indeed.

Inside of the lens there is a fluid as clear as water. In this fluid you see a sort of curtain with a round opening in it. This opening is called the pupil of the eye. It is not always of the same size. When there is a very bright light, it is small, but when the light is dim, it is large, for then you want all the light that you can get in that dark chamber. You can see the pupil change in its size if you look into the eye of anyone while you bring a light very near, and then move it away quickly.

Around the pupil is a curtain, which we call the iris. It is circular. Its outer edge is fastened all around to the inside of the eyeball. The same watery fluid in the lens is also on both sides of this curtain. It would not do to have the jelly here, for the curtain would not move easily while changing the size of its opening.

The color of the iris is different from person to person. When it is blue we say that the person has blue eyes, and if it is quite dark, we say that he has black eyes. The iris makes the eye very beautiful, but its chief use is, as you see, to regulate the amount of light that goes into the eye. When there is a great deal of light, the iris is drawn in such a way as to make the round opening very small. When there is little light, it is drawn so as to make this opening large. The iris must be made very well, or it would be puckered when the opening in it is changed in this way. No man could make a curtain of this shape, and expect it to work like this. It would be a very awkward thing if he should undertake it. He could not possibly make it so that the round opening in it could be made smaller and larger without wrinkling. But look at this beautiful curtain in the eye, and see how smooth it is;

how perfectly round its edge stays as the size of the pupil is changed. Did you ever see anything work more beautifully and easily than the iris does?

The opening in the curtain is different in different animals. In the cat it has this shape.

In the horse it is shaped in this way.

The pupil of the cat's eye is designed by God to be vertically lengthened, so that the creature may easily see things above and beneath. Their habits lead them either to look up or down; up to rocks or boughs of trees, or down to the ground if they are on the rocks or in a tree. Because the pupil is oval, lengthened upwards and downwards vertically, a cat can watch its prey without moving its head. The long pupil takes in all that is before it.

The eyes of horses and cattle-like creatures, which graze in fields, have horizontal pupils because the creatures require good vision on either side, so that no enemy may approach them unaware.

You can see the difference in the size of the cat's pupil in different lights. If you look at its eyes in the bright sunlight, and then again in the evening, you will see that the pupils are very much larger in the evening than they are in the day. When the sun is very bright, the cat's pupil is a mere chink. But in the evening it is very wide open to allow more light to pass through the lens.

But how do you see? How do the eyes work? The light

that goes in through the pupil makes an image or picture of everything that is before the eye. It makes the image on a very thin sheet spread out on the back part of the dark chamber of the eyeball. It is just as light makes images of things in a mirror, or in the smooth, still water. The only difference is that the image or picture in the eye is very small. When you see a tree reflected in the still water, the picture is as large as the tree itself. But the picture that the light makes of the tree in that dark chamber of your eye is very small. The picture in your eye of a whole landscape, with all its trees, houses, and hills does not cover a space larger than a dime.

We may better understand how images are pictured on the back of the dark chamber of the eye by a very simple experiment.

A simple picture can be produced in some dark shed that has no windows. Knotholes are sometimes seen, that are so circular and so smooth they produce the effect of a lens. Should a white sheet be placed on the side of the shed directly opposite the hole, the images of all that happen to pass before the hole outside are pictured, in the beautiful colors of nature, on the cloth. If you or a friend should stand outside, you would also be shown on the cloth. This is exactly what happens in our eyes when there is light enough to see. There is a picture of what is before our eyes, and that picture is cast onto the back part of the eye, on a network of nerves called the retina.

Photographs are taken in a similar way by a camera instead of a dark room. The photographer's camera is like the eye, and is an imitation of it. If we use a small box and put a glass lens into the hole, there will be a clearer picture cast onto the camera backing behind it. If we put a roll of film into the camera, the picture can be seen on the film. The film is coated with a special substance of bromide and nitrate of silver. This captures the picture, and when the film is developed, it is seen to be an exact copy of that which was placed before the hole in the box. This is a simple explanation of photography, the art of taking pictures by the use of the camera.

But how does the brain sense anything about these pictures? It senses them by means of a nerve that goes from the eye to the brain, and is spread out where the pictures or images are made. It would do no good to have the pictures made in the eye if the nerve could not tell the mind about them. The eye might be perfect, and yet you might not see anything. It is as necessary to have the nerve in good order as it is for the eye itself. It is not your eye that sees, it is your brain, and in seeing it uses both the nerve and the eye.

You have two eyes. When you look at something, for instance a house, there is a picture of the house in both eyes. The two nerves tell the mind in the brain about the two pictures. Why? Why doesn't the mind see two houses? It is because the pictures in the two eyes are almost exactly alike, and both nerves tell the same story. If they did not, then the mind would see two houses; that is, it would see double. You can see double by pressing one eye sidewise while you let the other go free, but it is foolish to press on your eyes at any time.

The eyes of insects are very different. They are like beautiful clusters of flowers known as compound flowers. As in a compound flower there are a great many flowers together, so it is with the eyes of insects. The eye of a common fly is made up of thousands of eyes; so, when it looks at anything, there are thousands of very little images made by the light in these eyes, and the nerves tell the fly's little brain about them. These eyes are very small. The nerves that go from them to the fly's brain must be very fine! Your eye is a very wonderful instrument, but God has put thousands of them just as wonderful into the head of the fly that buzzes about you. It is as easy for Him to make little eyes as large ones, and He can make a multitude as easily as one.

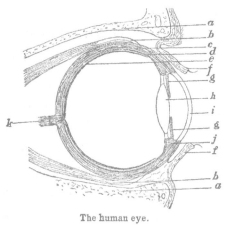

The human eye.

| | | |
|---|---|---|
| a bone of the orbit. | e retina. | i cornea. |
| b muscle which moves the eyeball. | f eyelid. | j muscle which changes the shape of the lens. |
| c sclerotic coat. | g iris. | |
| d choroid coat. | h lens. | k optic nerve. |

# Review

1. Through what senses does the brain gather the most information?

2. Describe the different parts of the eye. Be sure to include the white, the iris, the pupil, and the lens.

3. Why is the cat's pupil shaped vertically and the horse's shaped horizontally?

4. How is the photographer's camera similar to the eye?

5. How are images created in the eye?

6. Why do you have two eyes?

7. Describe the eyes of insects.

# How the Eye Is Guarded

The eye is a very tender organ. It is therefore guarded carefully, and is very seldom hurt even though it is right in the front part of the head. It must be there for you to use to see. And it is open much of the time. You would suppose that it may often be struck and hit by things that are thrown about. But it is really very seldom hit so as to be hurt much.

The parts around the eye are often injured, but the eye itself usually escapes injury. We often see the eyelids and the cheek black and blue from a blow, and yet the tender and delicate eye is as sound as ever. People say, in such cases, that the eye is black and blue, but this is not so; the injury is all on the outside, and does not go into the eye.

Let us see in what ways the eye is guarded. It is in a deep, bony socket. There is bone all around except in front. See also how the bones stand out all around it. The bone of the forehead juts over it. Below and to the outside the cheekbone stands out and the nose protects it on the inside. Now you can see that a blow with a stick would be very likely to strike upon one of these walls of bone, and the eye would then be unharmed. They are real walls of defense to the eye. A stick cannot hit the eye itself unless it goes with its end pointed directly at the eye. It must go in this way to avoid striking on these walls of bone, by which the eye is surrounded.

But if the stick gets by these bony walls, it still may not hurt the eye, after all. Perhaps you never thought what use there is in being able to wink so quickly. See what winking does. It shuts the eyelid over the eye, so that nothing can get into it unless it is something sharp enough to pierce through the lids. And a blow will not hurt the eye, if the lids are closed, unless it is hard enough to bruise it through the lids.

How quick is the working of that winking muscle! The moment that the eye sees anything that may injure it coming towards it, this muscle shuts up the eye out of sight as quick as a flash. It hardly seems as if there was time for a message to go from the eye to the brain, and then another back from the brain to that muscle in the lids. But all this happens. The nerve of the eye tells the brain of the danger, and the brain sends a message to the eyelid muscle. This is done so quickly that whenever people speak of anything as being done very quickly, they are very apt to say that it was done in the twinkling of an eye. This expression is used in the Bible, in 1 Corinthians 15:52.

But I have not told you all that this winking muscle does. It does something more than shut the eye in. It pushes it back in its socket, so that it is a little farther out of the way of a blow. And it does not push it right against the hard bone of the socket; there is a soft cushion of fat for it to press the eye against.

And this is not all. When the eye sees a blow coming, this muscle acts so strongly that it wrinkles the skin of the eyelids, and pulls down the eyebrow, and draws up the cheek, as you see here. This guards the eye. The cheek and the eyebrow are brought so near together that there is but little room for the blow to get at the eye; and even if it does, the wrinkled skin of the lids makes a cushion over it that breaks the force of the blow. You can see that the blow would be much more apt to do harm if the winking muscle merely brought the lids together. As it is, a blow usually hits on the eyebrow, or cheek, or both, while the eye is safe, shut up and pushed back in its cavern upon its cushion of fat. To see how much the bringing together of the cheek and eyebrow defends the eye, you must look at someone as he tightly closes the eye, as represented in the figure. And if, at the same time, you put your finger on the eyelid, you will see how the cushions that all this wrinkling makes over the eye and about its socket defend it from harm.

So you see that not only is the eye guarded by walls of bone, but the winking muscle also raises up cushions over them whenever the eye sees a blow coming. These cushions often save the bone from being cracked, and in this way also keep the eye from being hurt.

Of what use do you think the hairs on the eyebrows are? They are for good looks, you will say. But they are for something more than this; they are a defense to the eye. You know what the eaves of a house are for when there is no gutter to the roof—they keep the rain from running down from the roof on the sides of the house. They make it drop off to the ground a little way from the house. In a similar way the hairy eyebrows make the sweat of the forehead drop off upon the cheek, instead of running down into the eye. The eyebrows, then, are the eaves over the roof of the eye's house.

Perhaps you will ask what the sweat would do if it should run down into the eye. It would not feel very good because of the salt in your sweat. It would irritate the eye and make it red. The eye might become inflamed.

The eyelashes, besides making the eye look nice, are also a defense for it. You know that there are often small things flying about in the air, which cannot be easily seen. If these float toward the eye, they generally hit against the eyelashes, and are prevented from going into the eye.

Tears are also a defense for the eye. If anything happens to get by the eyelashes into the eye, the tears quickly flow to wash it out. Commonly the tear gland only makes enough tears to keep the eye a little moist; but as soon as anything gets into the eye and irritates it, the tear gland sets to work quickly, and produces tears. At the same time, the winking muscle keeps moving the lids, and what is in the eye is soon washed out.

Tears are flowing into the eye all the time. If they did not, the eyeball and the inside of the lids would become dry, and they would not move easily against each other. You would have to keep wetting them with water to prevent them from rubbing. The tear gland, which is just above the eye, through little tubes or ducts, continually sends down just enough tears to make this motion of the eye and the lids easy.

But you may ask where the tears go. They do not commonly run out over the lids, but they must go somewhere. If you look at the eyelids of anyone, you can see in each lid a little hole at the end of the edge towards the nose. The tears go into these holes, and down through a duct that ends in the nose. This duct is like the sink drain for the tears. After washing the eye, tears run off through it. The two little holes in the lids commonly take in all the tears as quickly as they come, but when we cry, the tear gland makes tears so fast that these holes cannot take them all in. The tears, therefore, overflow their banks — the lids — and run down on the cheek.

## Review

1. Why is the eye seldom injured?

2. What parts around the eye are often injured instead of the eye itself?

3. Describe how the bones around the eye defend it.

4. How does the winking muscle help to defend the eye?

5. What does it do besides covering the eye?

6. Describe how the eyebrows and eyelashes protect the eye.

7. Describe how tears work.

## Hearing

What is sound? If you look at a large bell when it is struck, you can see a quivering or shaking in it. If you put your hand on it, you can feel the quivering. It is this quivering that makes the sound we hear. You can see the same thing in the strings of a piano when they are struck and in the strings of a violin as the bow is drawn over them. The wind makes the music on the Aeolian harp in the window by shaking its strings. And when you speak or sing, the sound is made, as you have learned before, by the quivering of two flat cords in your throat.

But when a bell is struck, how does the sound get to our ears? The quivering or vibration of the bell makes a vibration in the air, and this vibration is carried along through the air to our ears.

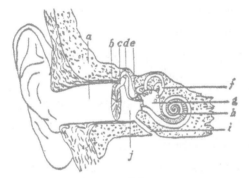

Diagram of the ear.

| | |
|---|---|
| *a* outer air passage. | *f* semicircular canals. |
| *b* membrana tympani. | *g* vestibule of inner ear. |
| *c* malleus, or hammer bone. | *h* cochlea. |
| *d* incus, or anvil bone. | *i* Eustachian tube. |
| *e* stapes, or stirrup bone. | *j* tympanum, or middle ear. |

The vibration can go through other things besides air. It will go through something solid better than it will go through air. Put your ear at the end of a long log, and let someone scratch with a pin on the other end. You can hear it very clearly. The vibration made by the pin travels through the whole length of the log to your ear. But if you take away your ear from the log you cannot hear it, for the vibration cannot come to you so far through the air.

The closer you are to where the sound is made, the louder it is. The farther the sound goes, the fainter it is. It is said to die away as it goes. The vibration becomes less and less until it is all lost. If you drop a stone into the water, it makes ripples in all directions. These become fewer and fewer the farther they go from where the stone was dropped. It is the same with the waves or vibrations of sound in the air.

What is an echo? It is when a sound that you make comes back to you again. It is done in this way. The vibration strikes against some rock, or house, or something else, and then bounds back to you, just as a wave striking against a rock bounds back.

Why is it that a person speaking in a building can be heard more easily than one speaking in the open air? It is because the vibrations are shut in by the walls. It is for the same reason that you can hear a whisper so far through a speaking tube extending from one part of a building to another. The vibrations are shut in within the tube. They have no chance to spread out in all directions, and they go right straight on through the tube.

You have learned how sound is made and how it goes through the air and through solids. How is it that we hear sound when it comes to our ears? How does the brain know anything about the vibration of the air? This vibration does not go directly into the brain, where the mind is; it only goes a little way into the ear, and there it stops. It vibrates against the drum of the ear, and can go no farther. How, then, can the brain sense it?

The vibration of the air goes into the ear to a membrane fastened to a rim of bone called the drum, and shakes it, and this shakes a chain of little bones that are on the other side of this drumhead. The last of these bones is fastened to another little drum, and, of course, this also vibrates. This drum covers an opening to some winding passages of bone. These passages are filled with a watery fluid. Now the shaking of the second little drum makes this fluid shake. The nerve of hearing feels this shaking of the fluid, and tells the brain.

Here are the four little bones that make up the chain of bones in the ear. They are curiously shaped. The one marked **a** is called the hammer, and **b** is called the anvil. The one marked **c** is called the stirrup. This is the bone that is fastened to the second drum — the one that covers the opening into the winding passages. The vibration that comes to the first drum is passed on by this chain of bones to the second drum.

See, now, how many different vibrations there are for every sound that you hear. First, the bell, or whatever the source of sound is, vibrates. Then there is a vibration of the air. This vibrates the eardrum. Then the chain of bones is vibrated. The farthest one of them vibrates another drum, and this vibrates the fluid in the bony passages. This happens every time you hear a sound, and when you hear one sound after another coming very quickly, the vibrations chase each other, as we may say, as they go into the ear! But they are not jumbled together. They do not overtake one another. Every vibration goes by itself, and so each sound is heard distinctly from the others, unless the vibrations come very fast indeed. Then they would make one continuous sound. Each puff of a loco-motive when it starts is heard distinctly. But as the loco-motive goes on, the puffs get nearer and nearer together, and when it goes very fast, they are so near together that the vibrations do not go separate into the ear, and they make a continual sound. In this way, the vibration of one sound gets into the fluid in the bony passages before the one that follows it.

As you have learned, sound spreads in all directions in vibrations or waves.  The more waves the ear catches the more distinct the hearing is. Some animals that need to hear very well have very large ears. Here is one, the long-eared bat. It must hear very well, for its mon-strous ears must catch a great many of the sound waves. We might hear better if our ears were larger; but large ears would probably not look very good on our heads, and we usually hear as well as we need.

Sometimes, when we do not hear as distinctly as we wish to, we put up the hand to the ear, as you see represented. This helps the hearing by stopping the waves of sound, and turning them into the ear. Those who are very deaf sometimes have a hearing aid. A hearing aid is an electronic device that amplifies the waves of sound so they can be heard.

Some animals can turn their ears so as to hear well from different directions. The horse quickly pricks up its ears when it sees or hears something that it wants to know more about, and then it can turn its ears backward when it wants to do so. It is in such timid animals as the hare, the rabbit, and the deer that we see the ears move the most. They are on the watch all the time for danger, and at the quietest sound that they hear they turn their ears in the direction of it. Their ears are large, so that they hear very easily.

You have learned how the eye is guarded. The ear is also well guarded. But it is the inner parts, where the hearing is really done, that really need to be so well guarded. You remember that there are passages in the ear that are filled with a fluid. The hearing nerve has its fine, delicate fibers in these passages. They feel the vibration of the fluid, and tell the brain of it. It is necessary that this part of the hearing system should be well guarded. For this reason, these passages are enclosed in the very hardest bone in the body.

The very entrance into the ear is well guarded, and in an

interesting way. The canal that leads to the drum of the ear is always open, and you know bugs can easily crawl into such holes. What do you suppose is the reason they do not often crawl into the ear? There is something there to prevent them. It is the earwax. They probably do not like the smell of it, and if they come to the entrance, they turn around. Once in a while a bug might go in, but it is prevented from doing much harm by the wax. The bug is soon covered with this wax, which is so sticky that the bug is kept from kicking very hard. And, after all, though the bug may cause some discomfort, it cannot get at the delicate part of the ear. It dies after a while, if it cannot get out, and perhaps the bitterness of the wax helps to kill it.

# Review

1. How is sound made?

2. How do sounds get to our ears?

3. Describe what happens when sound dies away.

4. What is happening when you hear an echo?

5. What happens when you speak into a tube?

6. How do we hear sounds?

7. Describe the little bones in the ear. What do these bones do?

8. Describe the different vibrations that take place in your ear.

9. How are your ears different from the ears of ani-

mals?

10. How is the inner part of the ear guarded?

11. What does earwax do?

---

# Smell, Taste, and Touch

You have learned that most of what the brain knows about the world around it comes to it by sight and hearing. But it learns a great deal through other senses you will learn about in this chapter.

Did you ever wonder how it is that you smell anything? You put a rose up to your nose, and the fragrance is pleasant to you. What is this fragrance? Is it something that goes up into your nose? You cannot see anything come from the rose. But in reality, very fine particles come from it. They are finer than the finest powder. They float about in the air and as you breathe, they flow with the air into your nostrils. Every scent that you smell is made of such particles.

But how do you think the brain knows anything about these particles when they come into the nose? It is in this way. In the lining of the nose are fine ends of the nerve for smell. The ends of the branches of this nerve are so small that you cannot see them. The fine scent particles touch these ends of the nerve, and the nerve tells the brain about them. This is how you smell.

The nose is a more complicated organ than most people think. There are divisions in it. These fold on each other in such a way that there is a great deal of surface in the nose, and the ends of the nerve of smell cover this surface.

Some animals have a very sharp sense of smell. The divisions in their nose are very large, and so the nerve spreads over a broad surface. The dog is able to track its master by smelling his footsteps. The cat, too, has a very keen smell for rats and mice.

Some people have a sharp sense of smell for certain things. There was a blind gentleman who could always tell by his sense of smell when there was a cat nearby. Once he was very sure that there was one nearby, though no one else could see it. He insisted that he was right, and after a while the kitten was found in a closet of the room.

The sense of smell can give us great enjoyment. The Creator has, for our enjoyment, scattered sweet-smelling flowers all over the earth. These are all perfume factories, made by Him for our pleasure and His glory. He could have made the flowers and fruits in such a way that they would have no smell, but in His desire to please us and make us happy, He has given to them a great variety of pleasant odors. There are, it is true, some unpleasant smells in the world, but these are not as common as the pleasant ones, and many unpleasant smells are very useful in warning us of danger.

The sense of taste is another source of gratification to us. The nerve of this sense has its fine ends mostly in the tongue. What we take into the mouth touches these ends of the nerve, and the nerve tells the brain about it. This is how you taste.

Besides the pleasure that we have from taste, the great use of this sense is to guide us in the choice of food. We choose the kinds of food that are proper for us by our taste. Creatures very seldom make a mistake in this. The sense of taste, like that of smell, sometimes warns us of danger. If our food tastes bad, we know that there is something wrong with it, and we do not eat it. Our sense of taste can sometimes help us from becoming sick.

The sense of touch gives a great deal of information to the brain. This sense has a large number of nerves in all parts of the body, and they are making reports continually to the brain. Especially busy in this way are the nerves of the tips of the fingers. It is by the fine ends of these nerves that the brain finds out how different things feel. It finds out whether they are soft or hard, smooth or rough.

Nerves in the tips of the fingers are of great service to the brain in guiding the use of muscles. In playing with the fingers on an instrument, the feeling in the ends of them is a guide to the brain in working them. So it is with anything that we do with them. You could not do some of the simplest things if there were no feeling in your fingers. You could not even button and unbutton your coat.

The nerves of touch are not placed on the surface of the skin. We actually have two layers of skin, an outer and an inner one. The nerves are in the inner layer, and are covered by the outer layer. This outer layer is very thin except on the sole of the foot and the palm of the hand. Because of its thinness it is called the scarfskin. It is this skin which is raised when you have a blister. Perhaps you know that it does not hurt to prick this when we want to let the water out. But if the needle touches the inner skin where the nerves are, you feel it very quickly.

The ends of the nerves of touch are arranged in rows on the tips of the fingers. When you touch anything, the nerves in the inner skin sense it through this scarfskin. This is so thin and soft that the nerves can feel through it. At the same time, it is a good protection. If it were not for this, the nerves would be affected too much by the rubbing of things against them. They could not even bear the air. If you had no scarfskin you would be in great discomfort all the time. You know how much pain you suffer if you rub off the skin anywhere. It is the scarfskin only that is rubbed off, and this exposes to the air the fine ends of the nerves in the inner skin.

Animals, such as the spider monkey, that have long tails, which they use for climbing, have no hair on the under-surface of the tail. This portion is very sensitive, and is designed to allow the creature to use it as a fifth hand. The prehensile-tailed monkeys are known to take eggs out of deep-seated nests in trees by the use of their clasping tails.

Each animal has instruments especially designed for it by the Creator. Animals that have hoofs cannot feel much with their feet. They have their sense of touch mostly in their lips and tongues. The elephant has this sense chiefly at the end of its trunk. There is not much feeling in the paws of dogs, or cats. The whiskers of the cat are feelers. There are nerves at the root of each of those long hairs, so when anything touches the whiskers, the cat knows it at once.

Insects have feelers extending out from their heads. Sometimes they are very long, as you see in this insect, called the ichneumon fly. We see insects touch things with these feelers as we do with our hands as they are going about. Bees can work in the darkness of their hives, guided by their feelers. Indeed, the bee will not work at all if its feelers are cut off. It does not seem to know what to do. Insects sometimes appear to tell each other things by their feelers. In every hive of bees there is a queen. If she dies, those that know about it buzz around very quickly, telling the other bees by striking their feelers with their own. Those that are told tell others, and thus the event is soon known all over the hive.

# Review

1. What is fragrance?

2. How does your sense of smell work?

3. How is your nose different from the noses of animals such as the dog?

4. How does the sense of smell give us enjoyment?

5. How does the sense of taste work?

6. How is the sense of taste useful to us?

7. How does the sense of touch work?

8. Where do you most use your sense of touch?

9. How do the nerves of touch help in using the muscles?

10. Describe the two layers of skin. Why is an outer layer needed?

11. Describe how some animals use their sense of touch.

# Chapter Five

# The Structure of the Body

## Bones

You learned in the last chapter how it is that the brain gathers information about the world around it through the senses. But the brain does more than just gather information. It does work as well, and it works through the muscles. When you see a man busily at work, his muscles are doing the work. The brain is directing them to work by the nerves that connect to them. How does his brain know in what way to direct them? It is by experience gained through the senses. He has seen people do the same kind of work, and they have taught him about it. His brain uses the muscles in the way it has learned through the senses.

You see, then, that the brain makes use of information it gathers through the senses to do work. In doing work it uses the muscles. Information, then, goes into the brain through the senses — they are its inlets. But that information is used by the muscles. If you had a body that had senses but had no muscles, you might know a great deal, but you could not do anything.

The parts of the body that are most often moved by the muscles are the bones, and you shall learn about these before you learn about the muscles.

When you bend your arm, your muscles make the bones in your forearm rotate on the bone in your upper arm. There is a joint at your elbow for this purpose. There are joints in many other parts of the body, allowing the muscles to move, one bone upon another. The joints of the bones are so designed to function for years without repair. They work smoothly throughout your life. It would be amazing if a joint in a machine should work all the time for seventy or eighty years even with no one to repair it. But no man ever made such a joint. Men must keep oiling the joints in machinery. If they did not, the joints would soon wear out. The joints of our bones need no such care from us. We never need to oil them as men oil machinery. They are very well made. The ends of our bones are tipped with a very smooth substance, and this is continuously maintained. The joints always keep themselves oiled with a special fluid produced by the body.

The bones are the framework of the body. They are to the body like metal spokes are to an umbrella, or timbers to a house. The bones make the body straight. You could not stand up if you had no bones. You would have to crawl like the worm. When you see a person bracing himself to pull or push, the bones are all pressed tightly against each other by the strong muscles.

The bones of the body have very different shapes and sizes. Let us look at some of them.

The bones of the head, represented here, make a sphere-shaped container. This is the skull, where your brain is held. Great care is taken to guard this upper room of the body well. Its hard walls are made very strong.

Look at this barrel-shaped set of bones that make the chest. The ribs go round it as hoops go round a barrel. They are joined to the spine in the back and the breastbone in front. They are joined to the spine in such a way that they move up and down as you breathe. You can feel them move upward if you put your hand on your chest as you take a full breath. Inside of the barrel-shaped set of bones are the heart and lungs. The ribs protect these vital organs.

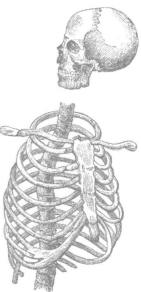

The spine is not only one bone; it is a chain or stack of twenty-four bones placed one above another. You can see a part of this stack, or column, in the figure of the bones of the chest. If it were all one bone, you could not twist your body about as you do. In bending over, you would not be able to bend your back. You could only bend your head forward on the top of the backbone, and bend your body forward on your lower limbs. That would be a very awkward movement. As it is, whenever you bend over, there is a little motion between each of the twenty-four bones, and this makes the movement easy and graceful.

The skull rests at the top of this column of bones. When you move your head backward and forward, it rocks on the top-most bone of this column. There are two little smooth places hollowed out on this bone for the skull to rock on, and the skull has two smooth rockers that fit into these hollowed places.

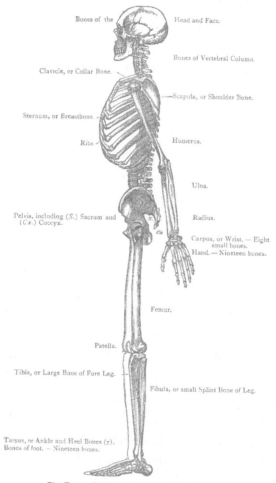

The Human Skeleton, showing position of bones.

# Review

1. How does the brain use the information it gathers?

2. What do you use to move your bones?

3. Why don't your joints wear out quickly?

4. What do the bones do for the body?

5. Describe the bones of the head.

6. Describe the bones of the chest.

7. How many bones are there in the spine?

8. Describe how the bones help the motion of the head.

# More About Bones

Here are the bones of the arm and the hand. At the top of the arm bone is a smooth round ball. It fits into a sort of cup. The joint here is what we call a ball-and-socket joint. The ball turns in the socket very easily in making any whirling motion with your arm, as you do when you jump rope.

The joint at the elbow is of a different kind. It is what we call a hinge joint. You cannot make any whirling motion at your elbow as you can at the shoulder; the motion is all one way, like a hinge.

There are a great many little bones in the wrist, hand,

and fingers. There is a very great variety in their motions so that the hand can do almost anything that you want it to do. You will learn more about this when you read the section about the hand.

Here are the bones of the leg and foot. You can see the knee joint and the lower end of the stout thigh-bone. They make a hinge joint with the large shin. The joint bends only one way, backward and forward, as it does when you walk. The small, thick bone, called the patella is not shown in the figure. One of the uses of this bone is to shield the joint. If you fall down, when running, you are likely to fall on your knee. This shield keeps the joint from being hurt.

There is a long, slender bone at the side of the large one. One might think that this would be very easily broken, but it is not because it is so well protected by muscles. Its lower end is quite thick and strong, and makes the outer part of an ankle. The ankle joint is a joint much like your wrist.

There are as many bones in the foot as there are in the hand. Why is this? You remember that the hand has so many bones because it has to perform so many different motions. It is the same with the foot. If the bones of the foot were joined at a simple hinge, the foot would be very stiff and clumsy, with no flexibility. Walking and running with such feet would be awkward.

The bones of different animals are made differently, according to the work they do. Those that do heavy work have heavy, stout skeletons, but those that do only light work have slender bones. A bird has a light skeleton, for it could not fly so well with a heavy one. Here is the skeleton of a bat. The bones are exceedingly light and slender, for flying is light and nimble work.

The bones of an adult are more brittle than those of a child. If the child's bones were brittle they would be very often broken because he so often tumbles down. If adults were as careless as children are, there would be broken limbs to be taken care of in almost every house.

There is one feature in the child's head that prevents the bones from breaking in his frequent falls. In the grown person the bones of the head are fastened tightly together, and are almost like one bone. But it is not so with the child. In an infant's head they are very loose, and you can feel quite a space between the bones at the top of his forehead. When the child falls and hits his head, the loose bones give and do not break.

Though the teeth seem similar to bones, they are different from them in one thing. The bones grow with the rest of the body, but the teeth never grow any larger after they first push up through the gum. The outside of the tooth — the enamel, as it is called — is very hard. This hardness is so the tooth may do its work well. Such a hard substance, after being made once, is finished. It never can grow any more. No blood can flow through it to make it grow, as it does in the bones.

Now you can understand the reason that every person has two sets of teeth. If the teeth that one has when a child should remain in his head, they would be too small for him when he became an adult. As the jaws grew they would become quite far apart, and so would look very strange. To take care of these difficulties, the first set begins to be shed at about the age of seven, and a new set of larger teeth takes its place. As the new teeth are not only larger, but are more in number, they fill up all the room designed for them in the enlarged jaws.

All the bones of our bodies are inside, and are covered with muscles, cords, and ligaments. Covering all this is the skin. But the bones of some animals are on the outside. This is the case with crabs and lobsters. Their bones make a sort of armor to defend the soft parts from being injured. The hard coats of many insects also may be considered as their skeletons. Outer skeletons are called exoskeletons.

Animals such as crabs and lobsters have new skeletons every year. The old skeletons are too small for their growing bodies, and so they must be cast off. The animal crawls into a quiet place to go through the process of shedding. It makes a great effort, and the shell comes apart. Then, by hard struggling, it pulls itself out. The creature now stays still a few days in its resting place, and another exoskeleton, as hard as the old one, is formed. When it comes out with its new armor on, it is as brave and as ready to fight as ever.

# Review

1. Compare the shoulder, elbow, knee, wrist and ankle joints.

2. What happens to the bones as they grow older?

3. Describe the bones in the head of a child.

4. How are the teeth different from the bones?

5. Why do we have two sets of teeth?

6. What sort of skeletons do crabs and lobsters have?

# Muscles

You have already learned a few things about muscles. They make all the motion in the body. They move the bones, as well as the tongue, the lips, and the eyes.

But how do they do this? Stretch a rubber band with your hands. Now let it go, and it will shorten itself. When a muscle pulls a bone, it shortens itself just as a rubber band does. But the cause of its shortening itself is different. The brain makes the muscle shorten. You think to bend your arm, and, as quick as thought, the message goes through nerves to the muscle, and it shortens itself to bend the arm.

Here is a figure that shows the muscle that bends the arm and the muscle that straightens it out. All the other muscles of the arm are left out, so that you may see how these operate. Look at the muscle marked **a**. You can see that  when this shortens itself it must pull up the forearm. The muscle **b** has the opposite effect. The end of this muscle is fastened to the point of the elbow, and when it shortens it pulls the forearm down and straightens the arm.

When a muscle shortens itself, it bulges out and becomes hard. Straighten your arm, and take hold of it with your other hand a little above the elbow. Now bend up your arm as forcibly as you can, and you will feel the muscle on the front of the arm swell out and harden.

The muscles are the fleshy part of the body. The meat of animals is made up of muscles. They are not of the same color in all animals. In some they are quite red, while in others they are of a light color. Beef — the meat of the ox or the cow — is a deep red, and is very different from the meat of a fowl. The muscles of fishes are generally very light in color.

The forearm is very fleshy. Most of the muscles that move the fingers, as well as those that move the hand, are in the forearm. Take hold of that part of the arm with your other hand while you work the fingers back and forth, and you will feel the muscles as they shorten themselves to pull the fingers. Here is a figure showing the muscles in this fleshy part of the arm. You can see that they are quite large. The wrist is very slender in comparison. There are no muscles there. Instead, bright, shining, smooth cords are in the wrist running from the muscles to the fingers. These cords are called tendons. The muscles pull the fingers by these tendons just as men pull at pulleys by ropes. You can see the play of these cords very well on the back of the hand as the fingers are worked.

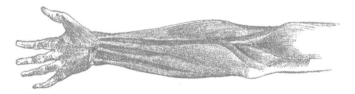

There are some very small muscles in the hand, such as those that spread the fingers out and those that bring them together again. If you work your fingers in this way, you will see that these muscles, which do such light work, need not be very large. The muscles that do the hard work of the hand are up in the arm. They are very large. If they were not, you could not grasp things so tightly, and pull as hard as you might sometimes need.

Why is it that these large muscles are so far away from where they do their work? If they were in the hand, they would be large and clumsy. They are therefore higher up in the arm and use small, but very strong cords to pull the fingers. They give the arm the round fullness that makes its shape so beautiful.

You can see the same kind of arrangement in the drum-stick of a chicken. The large muscles that work the claws are up in the full, round part of the leg, and there are small, stout cords that extend from them down to the claws. Children who live on a farm sometimes amuse themselves by pulling these cords in the drum-stick of a fowl, making the claws move the same way the animal would have moved the muscle when it was alive.

As it is with the muscles that move the fingers, so it is with the muscles that move the toes. They are mostly up in the leg, and the slender tendons, by which they pull, run down over the ankle to the toes, just as in the arm, the tendons go over the wrist to the fingers. If the muscles for toe movement were all in the foot, they would be very clumsy, and the leg would be ugly for lack of fullness.

The tendons at the wrist and ankle are bound down very tightly. If this were not so they would be always falling out of place, stretching out the skin before them in ridges. This would be the case especially with the tendons at the ankle. Every time the muscles pulled on them, they would bulge out at the bend of the ankle if they were not held firmly in place by the ligaments.

The muscles are of many shapes — round, flat, long, and short. They are shaped to suit the work they are designed to do.

They vary much in size as well as shape. Some are very large, and some are small. How large are the muscles of the arm that wield the hammer and the axe! But how small are the muscles that work the musical cords in your throat when you speak or sing! These little muscles make all the different notes of the voice by pulling on these cords, and many of their motions are very slight.

You remember that in the chapter on hearing you learned about the little bones in the ear. These use very small muscles that move them. The bones and the muscles, **a** and **b**, are represented in the following figure. Both the bones and the muscles are larger in this figure than they are in the body. The muscles have tendons to pull by, in the same way that the muscles in the arm have. As the bones are the smallest ones that we have, so it is with the muscles. This part of the hearing system is very small.

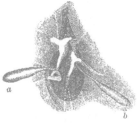

The birds that fly swiftly on their wings have very large muscles to work them. This gives them their full, round breast. But the muscles that work the musical cords in their little throats, as they sing so sweetly, are so small that it is difficult to see them.

# Review

1. How is all the motion of the body made?

2. Describe how the muscles move the different parts of the body.

3. Explain how the muscles of the arm work.

4. What happens to the muscles as they shorten or lengthen?

5. What is the meat of animals made up of? Describe the colors of meat in the various animals.

6. Describe the muscles in the forearm, wrist, and hand.

7. Describe the function of tendons and ligaments.

8. Describe the muscles that birds use for flying and singing.

---

# More About Muscles

There are a great number of muscles in the whole body to produce all its motions. There are about fifty in each arm. In the whole body there are about four hundred and fifty, and each muscle is made up of a great number of fibers or threads, each fiber having its own work to do.

All these muscles have nerves that connect them to the brain, which tells them by these nerves just what to do. Each muscle has a great many little nerve endings scattered through it. The message from the brain that tells the muscle to act does not go to the whole muscle, as a message is sent to a person. It goes to each nerve, telling that fiber what to do. Every fiber of the muscle has its little nervous tube connecting it to the brain, for the nerves are bundles of tubes, just as the muscles are bundles of fibers. Each fiber gets its messages from the brain by its own separate tube, so that each fiber is a worker by itself. How well these workers pull together when they all get a message from your brain by the nerves!

It usually takes several muscles to make any motion, and sometimes many muscles act together. When this happens, messages are sent to a great multitude of fibers in these many muscles. Raise your hand. It is not one muscle that does this, but many. Your brain has sent a message to all the fibers of these muscles, and they have all done their part in raising your hand. Now raise it again, this time a little differently. A different message for this has been sent to all the fibers. So for all the different motions there are different messages. It is amazing that so many different messages can be sent through the nerves to the fibers of all the muscles, and that these fibers should obey them so perfectly.

This is wonderful even in so simple a motion as raising the hand, but how much more wonderful it is when a great variety of rapid motions are made by the muscles, as when one plays a piano! How busy the brain of the player is in sending its messages, one after the other, to the multitude of muscle fibers that work the arms and fingers! If the musician sings at the same time that he plays, his brain is sending messages also to the muscles of the chest, throat, and mouth. It is even more wonderful that even as the brain is sending out so many messages, it is receiving messages from the senses. Messages are being received from the sounds of the piano and the voice along the nerves of the ear. They go also from the tips of the fingers as they press the keys. How wonderful that all these messages are going back and forth so rapidly, and the brain can manage them without any confusion!

You have learned that there are some parts besides bones that are moved by muscles. They move different parts of the face, and it is this that creates different expressions. Thus, when you are amused to laughter, the muscles pull up the corners of the mouth. If you laugh very hard, they pull them up very much, as you see in the face drawn here. See how this face is wrinkled under the  eyes. This is because the muscles pull at the corners of the mouth so hard as to push up the cheeks.

There are muscles to pull the corners of the mouth down, and these make the face look sad. If the muscles that wrinkle the eyebrows act at the same time, the face is both sad and angry, as you see here. Observe just what the difference is between this face and the smiling face. The difference is merely in the corners of the mouth and in the eyebrows. In this face the two wrinkling muscles of the eyebrows are in action, and so are the two muscles that pull down the corners of the mouth. Four small muscles make this face sad and angry. But in the smiling face the eyebrow-wrinkling muscles are relaxed, and the corners of the mouth are pulled up instead of down. It is the two little muscles that pull up the corners of the mouth that do all the smiling in the face.

You may have heard the expressions, "He had a down look," or "His countenance fell." These refer to the effect produced by sadness on the corners of the mouth. This also explains the meaning of the common expression, "Down in the mouth."

There is a certain muscle called the "proud" muscle. It pushes up the under lip. It is by this that pouting, that ugly expression so common with some children, is done. When the eyebrow-wrinkling muscles act at the same time, a scowl is combined with the pouting expression, and then the face becomes very ugly indeed. We must not get into the habit of using these muscles foolishly. By God's grace, we must strive to be pleasant and kind, and then those nice little muscles that draw up the corners of the mouth will always be ready to light up your face with a cheerfulness that is consistent with Christian contentment.

There are some animals that have certain muscles in the face that we do not have. These are the snarling muscles. They pull up the lip at the sides of the mouth so as to show the long, tearing teeth. You can see them in dogs, tigers, and other wild animals when they are angry. No being but man has the frowning, or the sad, or the smiling muscles in the face. Perhaps you may say that the dog smiles when it is pleased and looks up at its master. A dog may seem to smile, it is true, but it does this only with its wagging tail, for it has no muscles in its face to smile with.

How wonderful is the variety of expression in the human face! And yet all are formed by a few muscles. The principal ones are those that draw up and draw down the corners of the mouth, and those that wrinkle the eyebrows.

Man does more things with his hand than with any other part of his body. You will now learn about the hand, and then about those things that various animals use somewhat like hands.

# Review

1. How many muscles are there in the arm and hand?

2. How many are in the whole body? What are they made up of?

3. Describe the structure of muscle fibers.

4. Describe what happens when the arm is raised in different ways.

5. What gives the face its various expressions?

6. Describe how the muscles help form the various expressions.

7. How are the muscles in the faces of animals different from those in the faces of people?

# The Hand

Man is the only being that has a hand. The monkey has something like a hand, but if you watch it as it picks things up, you will see that it is very awkward compared to your hand.

The hand is a wonderful instrument. Let us look at some of the things that the hand can do. See the construction worker wielding the heavy hammer. How strongly his hand grasps the handle! The fingers and thumb are bent by the large muscles in the arm. Now these same fingers that grasp the hammer so strongly and do this heavy work can be trained to do work of the lightest and finest kind. They can take hold of the pen and write. They can move the tool of the engraver, making fine lines. In the machines that man makes, there can be no changing from coarse and heavy work to that which is fine and delicate. No man ever made a machine that would pull a large rope one moment, and the next pull a fine thread, and do the one just as well as the other. But that wonderful part of your body, the hand, can do this. It can grasp the rope firmly, and yet can take between its thumb and finger a thread so fine that you can hardly see it.

But the difference in the work of the hand is not merely in coarseness and fineness. It can do many different kinds of coarse work and a great many different kinds of fine work. The hand works very differently with various things. See how differently it manages a rope, a hammer, a spade, a hoe, a knife and fork. It takes hold of them in different ways. And then, in fine work, see how differently it manages a pen, an engraver's tool, a thread, or a needle. If you watch people as they do different things, you can get some idea of the variety of the work that the hand can perform. See how differently the fingers are continually placed as one is playing on an instrument. You can see very well the variety of shapes the hand can be put into if you observe a deaf person talking with his fingers. Following is a representation of the different ways in which the letters are made.

TALK WITH YOUR HANDS

The "j" is made by raising the little finger as represented, and then sweeping down to make the tail of the letter. The "z" is made by raising the forefinger, and moving it in a zigzag way.

The most common things that we do with our hands are really wonderful. Watch someone as he is buttoning up his coat. His fingers easily do it, and yet it is a wonderful performance. Suppose a man should try to make a machine that would do the same thing shaped like the hand. Do you think that he would succeed? Suppose that after working a long time he did succeed, and you saw his machine, with its fingers and thumb, put a button through a buttonhole in the same way that you do it with your fingers. Do you think that it could manage buttons of all sizes, large, and small? No, it could only button those that are of one size. The different sized buttons would require different machines. But your hand is a machine that, besides buttoning and unbuttoning buttons of various sizes, is continually doing a great variety of things that man-made machines cannot do. When some ingenious man makes a machine that can do any one thing like what the hand does, it excites our wonder, and we say, "How curious! How wonderful! How much like a hand it works!"

But the hand is not merely a machine that performs a great many motions. It is also an instrument with which you feel things. And what a delicate instrument it is for this purpose! How small are the things that you sometimes feel with the tip of your finger! As you pass it over a smooth surface, the slightest texture is felt. A great deal of information is gathered through the tips of your fingers. The nerves send messages from them continually to the brain. The blind read with their fingers. They pass them over raised letters, and the nerves of the fingers tell the brain what shape the letters are, just as the nerves of your eyes are now telling your brain what shape the letters are in this book.

While the hand is performing its different motions as an instrument, it is generally very much guided by this sense of touch. If your hand had no feeling, it would make even such a simple operation as buttoning awkward business, and you would not be able to button at all if you did not watch carefully while you were doing it. Your eye nerves would have to take the place of your finger nerves, as the finger nerves take the place of the eye nerves for the blind. As it is, you need not look at your fingers while they are buttoning, for they are guided by the sense of touch.

There was once a woman who lost the use of one arm, and also lost all her feeling in the other. She had a baby to care for. She could hold it with the arm that had no feeling, because she could work the muscles in that arm, but she could not do it without looking at her arm all the time. If she looked away, the arm would stop holding the baby and let it fall, for it could not feel anything. In her case the eye nerves had to keep watch in place of the arm nerves.

You see that the hand is different from the machines that man makes in two ways — in the variety of things that it can do, and in the connection that it has to the brain through the nerves. While the brain, through the nerves, controls the hand, the brain knows by other nerves all the time whether the hand is doing things right.

Look at the parts of this wonderful part of your body. The hand and arm have thirty bones, and about fifty muscles. All these are connected to the brain by nerves. It is through nerves that the brain makes the muscles perform all the various motions of your hand and fingers, and it is through other nerves that your brain is told what is felt in any part of your hand.

You have learned in this chapter a few of the things that you do with your hand, but there is no end to the things that can be done by this part of the body. You can get some idea of this in two ways — by moving your hands and fingers about in all sorts of ways and by thinking of the different things that people, in work or in play, do with their hands.

# Review

1. What animal has something like a hand? How does it compare with your hand?

2. Describe some kinds of work that the hand can do, both coarse and fine.

3. How can blind people read?

4. How does the hand work as an instrument of feeling?

5. How is the hand different from the machines made by man?

# Chapter Six
# *Animal Forms and Functions*

## In Place of Hands

Though animals do not have hands, they have different parts that they use to do some of the same things that we do with our hands. A dog might drag a rope along, which it holds in its mouth. It is making its teeth work in place of hands. Dogs always do this when they carry things. They cannot carry things in any other way. You carry a basket along in your hand, but the dog takes it between its teeth because it has no hands.

You have learned in another chapter how the cow and the horse crop the grass. They do it with their front teeth. They take up almost any kind of food with these teeth. These teeth work as hands for the cow and the horse. Their lips have also the same purpose in many cases. The horse gathers oats into its mouth with its lips. The lips serve as hands for such animals in another respect. They feel things just as we do with the tips of our fingers.

Monkeys have four things similar to hands. They are like a cross between hands and feet. With these they are very skillful at climbing. There are some kinds of monkeys, as the one shown, that use their tails in climbing as a sort of fifth hand.

The cat sometimes uses its paws for hands, sometimes its teeth, and sometimes both together. It climbs with its claws. It catches things with them — mice, rats, or anything that you hold out for it to chase. It strikes with its paws, when bothered or teased. When the cat moves its kittens from one place to another it picks them up with its teeth by the nape of the neck. There is no other way in which it can carry them. The cat cannot walk on its hind feet and carry kittens with its forepaws. It seems as if it would hurt a kitten to carry it in this way, but it does not.

When a squirrel nibbles a nut to crack a hole, it holds it between its two forepaws like hands. So also does the dormouse, which you see here.

The bill of a bird is used like a hand. It gathers food with it to put into its crop. When you throw corn out to the hens, how fast they pick it up, and send it down into their crops to be well soaked! The hummingbird has a very long bill, and in it lies a long, slender, and very delicate tongue. As it poises itself in the air before a flower, its wings fluttering so quickly that you cannot see them, the hummingbird thrusts its bill into the bottom of the flower where the nectar is.

The hummingbird moth, a kind of night butterfly, looks so much like a real bird that some people mistake one for the other. There are some hummingbirds that are but a little larger than a bumblebee, and the hummingbird moth is twice that size. The resemblance between the hummingbird moth and some common hummingbirds, in size, form, flight, flitting, and humming, is very great. The way each approaches a flower and hovers over it is also much the same.

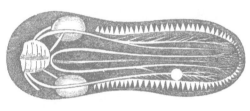

The bill of the duck is made in a peculiar way. It gets its food under water in the mud. It cannot see what it picks up. It has to work altogether by feeling, and it has nerves in its bill for this purpose. Here is a picture of its bill, showing the nerves branching out on it. You see, too, a row of pointed ridges all around the edge. They look like teeth, but they are not teeth. They are used by the duck to find its food. It works in this way: it thrusts its bill down. And, as it takes it up, it is full of mud. Mixed with the mud are the things that the duck eats. The nerves tell the duck what is food, and it lets all the rest go out between the ridges. It is a sort of sifting operation, the nerves in the sieve of the bill taking good care that nothing good escapes.

One of the most remarkable grasping tools is the trunk of the elephant. The variety of functions in which the elephant uses this organ is wonderful. It can strike very heavy blows with it. It can wrench off branches of trees, or even pull up trees by the roots, by winding its trunk around to grasp them, as you see it doing here. The trunk is the elephant's "arm" with which it carries its young. It is amusing to see an old elephant carefully wind its trunk around a newborn elephant, and carry it gently along.

But the elephant can also do some very detailed things with its trunk. You see in this picture that there is a sort of finger at the very end of the trunk. It is a very nimble finger, and with it this monstrous animal can do a great variety of little things. The elephant will use its trunk to grasp and put into its mouth little bits of bread and other kinds of food that you hand to it. It can pick up a coin from the ground as easily as you can with your fingers. It is with this finger that the elephant feels things as you do with your fingers. I once saw an elephant take a whip with this fingered end of his trunk, and use it as handily as his trainer,

very much to the amusement of the spectators.

The elephant can reach a considerable distance with its trunk. And this is necessary because it has such a short neck. It could not get at its food without its long trunk. Observe, too, how it can turn this trunk about in every direction and twist it about in every way. It is really a wonderful organ, for it has over thirty thousand little muscles in it. All this army of muscles receives its orders through nerves from the brain.

You see that there are two holes in the end of the trunk, the elephant's nostrils. Into these it can suck water, and thus fill its trunk like a hose. Then it can turn the end of this trunk into its mouth and let the water run down its throat. But sometimes the elephant uses the water in its trunk in another way. It blows the water out through its trunk with great force. It does this when it wants to wash itself, directing its trunk in such a way that the water will splash over its back. The elephant sometimes blows the water out in play, for even such great animals have games. Sometimes it blows the water on people that it does not like.

There is a story of a tailor who pricked the trunk of an elephant with his needle. The elephant, as he was passing, put his trunk into the shop window, hoping that the tailor would give him something to eat. He was angry at being pricked, and was determined to make the man sorry for doing such an unkind act. As his keeper led him back past the same window, he poured upon the tailor his trunk-full of dirty water, which he had taken from a puddle nearby.

## Review

1. How can the dog carry things about?
2. What do cows and horses have in place of hands?
3. What does the cat have in place of hands?
4. What do hummingbirds feed on?
5. How does the duck use its bill?
6. Describe the structure and some functions of the elephant's trunk.

## Variety in Animals

You have seen what a variety of curious machinery there is in our bodies. You have learned some information about animals as well. There is a great deal of machinery in animals, and it is different in each species. The variety is wonderful. You see that the world is full of many kinds of animals, making it a very busy world. Have you ever thought of how different they are from each other?

See what a difference there is between man and animals. Look at the oyster. It lives in the water, shut up in its rough shell. It is not a traveler. It has no eyes to see with and no sense of smell. But it does have taste for its food. It has a sense of touch as well. The oyster has this, both to manage its food and to guard itself against harm. It does not move about much; it has no feet or hands, and it has but few muscles. It has one muscle to shut up its shell tight, when it is alarmed. Its brain and nerves are very small, for the oyster has but few functions to perform.

There is little complexity in an oyster, when you compare it with your body. But there is still considerable complexity even in the oyster. It has systems for digesting its food. It has circulating systems — a heart with arteries and veins. And it has gills like a fish, by which it gets oxygen from the air in the water. It has muscles, nerves, and a sort of brain.

Look, now, at another animal that has even less complexity in it than the oyster. Look at the hydra. This is a very little animal that is found in ponds, clinging to straws or sticks with a sort of sucker. Here is a picture of it. The small figure shows it in its natural size. The larger figure on the next page shows it as magnified by a microscope. This animal is little more than a stomach with long arms. We can turn its body inside out, and the animal will do just as well as before. The arms are merely for catching things, such as worms and insects, which it puts into the mouth of its stomach. One of the arms in the picture has caught something, which it is about to put into its mouth. When the little creature is alarmed, it gathers up all its arms around its stomach, and looks like a little ball. No brain has ever been discovered in it, but it is plain that it gathers and processes information in catching its food, and it gathers itself into a ball to escape notice.

Here is one of the arms of this animal as seen through a powerful microscope. It is made up of little cells or bladder-like things. How it is that the hydra makes the different motions of its arm, we do not know.

The two animals that you have just read about are very unlike man, but they are not much different than a multitude of others. The variety in the shapes of animals and in the arrangements of their different parts is almost endless, but with all this variety, all are alike in some things.

The variety of animals is so great that when one undertakes to study them, he continually finds something new. But one thing is always true of the machinery in animals — it is perfectly designed. It is always exactly fitted to do just what it has been designed to do. No machinery that man ever made is equal to it.

Animals are suited in their shapes and arrangements to the way in which they live. Some are made to fly. As you see if you look at the birds and insects that fly through the air, these have wings that exhibit great variety. Some animals are made to live in the water. Most of these have broad tails and fins fit for swimming, but some crawl like the crab. Some float about like the hydra, and some lie still like the oyster.

Some animals walk about on the ground. Man is the only being that walks about erect upon two feet. The beasts are four-footed. The monkey is one of the most singular of beasts. It has neither feet nor hands, but some things which are like both. With these the monkey is more of a climber than a walker. There are many small animals that walk on many feet. Snakes, without any feet, crawl along the ground. Some animals hop, as the frog and toad. Some travel by jumping, as the grasshop-per and the troublesome little flea, which is shown here, as magnified by the microscope. This animal must have very strong muscles to enable it to make such leaps with its long, crooked legs.

The more an animal moves, the more muscles it needs to make its motions. God gives to each animal just the machinery that it needs. Some have machinery that others do not have. Some have very little, while others have a great deal. In our bodies there is a great variety of machinery, for we are designed to do very many things.

# Review

1. Describe the various functions of the oyster.

2. Describe the hydra.

3. In what things are all animals alike?

4. How does the machinery in animals compare to tools made by man?

5. Name some animals that fly, some that swim, and some that walk.

6. Name some animals that hop and some that crawl.

7. For what sort of activity is the monkey especially suited?

# Animal Tools

Man is the only being that makes tools to use. God has given him a mind that can design tools, and He has also given him hands by which he can use them. But He has given no such mind to the animals.

Though the animals do not make tools, they have tools that they can use. God has already given them all the tools they need. Let us look at some of the tools that we find in different animals.

Think of a man in the stern or back end of a small boat. He is sculling, as it is called. He is making the boat go by working the oar to one side and then the other. The oar is the tool or instrument by which he does it. A fish has a tool like this, by which it goes through the water. Its tail is like the sculling oar that man has invented. If you watch the fish as it swims through the water, you will see that it moves its tail to one side and the other as the man does his oar. While the fish moves forward by means of its tail, it uses its fins mostly as balancers to guide its motion. It moves them rather gently except when it changes its course quickly. When the fish is moving along fast, and wants to stop, it makes its fins stand out straight on each side. This is just as rowers in a boat use their oars when they want to stop the boat.

Think of a man drilling a hole in a rock. You can hear the sound of the tool as it goes *clack, clack*, all the while. The woodpecker has a drill that works in the same way. With its bill it drills holes in the trees, and you can hear the sound of its tool just as you do with the rock-blaster. It is a sort of knocking sound repeated very quickly many times.

Why do you think that the woodpecker drills holes? It is to get at worms and insects, which the woodpecker eats. These live in the bark and wood of dead trunks and branches of trees. The woodpecker can hear them with its sensitive hearing, and drills to find them. It does not drill into live bark and wood, for it can hear no worms or insects there.

But the woodpecker's instrument is more than a drill. It is a drill with another tool inside of it. This tool is for pulling out the insect or worm that the woodpecker finds when drilling. It is shown in the following figure. It is a very long, straight tongue, and the tip is like a bony thorn. This is, as you see, armed with sharp teeth pointing backward, like the barbs of a fishhook. Here are, then, two instruments or tools together. And this is the way that the woodpecker uses them. While it is drilling, the two

parts of the bill are closed together, making a good wedge-pointed drill, and at the same time a snug case for the insect-catching tongue. As soon as the woodpecker finds an insect, it opens the drill and pushes the barbed end of its long tongue against the insect, drawing it into its mouth.

As the woodpecker has to strike so hard in drilling, the bones of its skull are made very heavy and strong. If this were not so, the drilling would jar its brain too much.

Another thing can be observed. While the woodpecker is drilling it needs to stand very firmly. It must hold on tightly to the tree, or it will slip as soon as it begins to drill. It has, therefore, 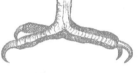 such claws as you see here to hold onto the surface of the tree.

Some animals have tools for digging. The elephant has long, strong tusks. These it uses for digging up different kinds of roots to eat. The hen digs with the claws of its feet to find grains and other kinds of food that may be mingled with the earth. The pig can dig with its snout. It does not have much use for this when shut up in its pen, but if you let it out, you will see how it roots, as we say. It does this to find food in the ground. When the pig runs wild, it roots to get acorns and other things that are buried in the earth.

The mole has a tool to work with, similar to the pig's. This animal has heavy claws with which it ploughs and digs. Here is a figure showing  the bones of one of its forepaws. They are very heavy and strong, and are worked by large muscles. The claws on its fingers are very powerful. The mole does great excavation with this digging and ploughing machine when making tunnels and galleries in the ground.

The mole's underground home is unique. It consists of a large circular room with several galleries and passages.  This is how it makes all this. It first heaps a round hill or mound, pressing the earth to make it very solid and firm. It then digs out a round room and then the passages. You can understand how the mole arranges these by the figure. You can see that there are two circular galleries, one above the other, and these are connected together by five passages. The circular room is connected with the upper gallery by three passages. It also has a deep passage at the bottom, which opens into a passage that leads from the lower gallery. This passage, and another like it on the other side, leads out into the open air. The purpose of all these winding passages is to enable the mole to escape from those who want to catch it.

The marmot, or woodchuck, as it is commonly called, is a great digger. It digs its hole in this way. It first loosens the dirt with its forepaws, using its teeth where the earth is very hard, or where any roots happen to be in the way. It pushes back the dirt as it loosens it.

Beavers are very unique. They do not live alone, but many of them often live together. They live in a sort of thatched hut, which they build with branches of trees, using mud, to hold it together like mortar. When gathering the branches they often gnaw them off with their sharp and powerful teeth. They are great diggers. They dig up the earth with their paws to use in building their home.

The beavers build their home at the water's edge, and the entrance to it is beneath the surface, so that they have to go under water to get to it. A dam is built to keep the water over this entrance at the proper level. If it were not for the dam, the door to the hut might get frozen over with ice if the water level should drop during the winter. The beaver builds the dam of tree branches, mud, and stones. The stones are used to hold the branches down. In the cabin there are two rooms. The upper room is where they live, and the lower room is where they store food for the winter. In the summer they do not live together in companies. Instead each one makes a burrow for itself. Every autumn they come together and unite in building their dams and thatched huts.

# Review

1. Why do people make tools and animals do not?

2. How is the swimming of a fish like sculling?

3. How does a fish use its fins?

4. How does the woodpecker use its bill?

5. What special structure enables the woodpecker to work safely?

6. How do elephants, hens, and pigs dig in the ground? Why do they dig?

7. Describe how the beaver constructs its home.

---

# More Animal Tools

Insects have various tools or instruments. There is a fly called the sawfly, because it has a saw. It is a very nice one, much nicer than any saw that man ever made. The fly uses the saw to make a place to put its eggs, where they will be secure. It also has a sort of glue with which it fastens the eggs in place.

Some insects have cutting instruments, which will cut as well as you can with scissors, if not even better. There is a bee that is remarkable in this respect. It has also a boring tool. Its nest is commonly built in old, half-decayed wood. It clears out a space in the wood using its boring tool. It then sets itself to work with its cutting instrument to cut out leaves to line the nest and build the cells. These are cut into different shapes, as they are needed, as you may see in the next picture. Below the leaves you see the nest. It is opened by removing some of the wood, and there you see the lining of leaves. Great pains are taken by the bees to make each leaf just the right shape so the pieces will be very nicely fastened together.

Some animals have machinery for making things. All the silk in the world is made by worms. The silkworm has a regular set of tools for spinning silk. It winds the tiny threads up as it spins them. Then man unwinds it and makes a great variety of beautiful fabrics with this silk thread.

The spinning tools of the spider are much finer than those of the silkworm. The thread that it spins is made up of many tiny threads. Each one of these runs from a tiny hole in the spider's body. The spider's web is a rope that it walks on like a ropewalker. You may sometimes see it swinging upon this thread. Sometimes, too, it lets itself down from some height, spinning the thread that holds it as it goes down. When the spider does this its spinning machine must work very briskly.

The paper wasp has special tools for making paper. It makes its paper out of fibers of wood, which it gathers into a bundle. It makes this into a soft pulp by mixing it with its own saliva. From this, the wasp makes the paper to build its nest. It is very much like the common brown paper that man makes. Wasps work in companies, and though each one can make but little paper, all together they make their nest in a short amount of time. The pulp from which they make their paper is very much like the pulp from which man makes paper, which you may see in the large tubs or vats of a paper factory. This pulp is made from wood that has been finely ground up.

Animals cannot use knives and forks to cut and divide their food. Instead they have instruments given to them, which do this very well. Those long, sharp teeth that dogs, cats, bears, and other beasts have are used to tear the flesh they eat, as thoroughly as we can cut it up. We do not need such teeth, because with instruments invented by man's mind for his hands to use, we cut up the food sufficiently.

You have learned that the elephant can draw up water into its trunk. Its trunk is like the straw with which we suck up water or any other liquid. And it is like a pump too, for water is raised in the pump just as it is in a tube

when we suck through it. It is with a pump similar to the elephant's that many insects drink the nectar from flowers. This little pump is called a proboscis. It is with such an instrument that the female mosquito sucks blood. At the end of its pump are sharp blades with which it cuts a hole in the skin before pumping the blood into its stomach. In some insects, such as the butterfly, the proboscis is very long. It is hollow, and with it the insect sucks up the nectar from very long flowers without having to climb to the bottom of them.

The proboscis is commonly coiled up when it is not in use. Here is the coiled proboscis of a butterfly. Two long feelers rise out over it.

The tongue of a cat is a unique instrument. It is rough like a hairbrush. When it cleans itself so carefully, it licks off the dirt and smoothes its coat just as the horse owner cleans and smoothes the horse's coat with a comb. It cannot reach its head with its tongue, so it has to use its forepaws instead.

There are some birds that eat fish. They have tools for catching them. The heron is a bird of this kind. When the light is dim, either at dawn or when there is moonlight, it is the heron's time for fishing. It will stand, as you see here, in shallow water, so stiff and still that it might be mistaken for the stump of a tree. It looks steadily and patiently into the water, and the moment it sees a fish comes along,

down goes its sharp bill, and off it flies to its nest with its prey. The plumes of this bird are beautiful, and were once very highly prized as ornaments.

There is one bird that lives mainly on oysters. It has a bill with which it can open an oyster shell as skillfully as an oysterman can with his knife.

Some birds can sew with their beaks and feet. There is one bird that sews so well that it is called the tailor bird. Here we see its nest hidden in leaves, which it has sewn together. It does this with thread that it makes. It gathers cotton from the cotton plant, and with its long, delicate bill and little feet, it spins the cotton into a thread. It then pierces holes through the leaves with its bill, and, passing the thread through the holes, sews them together.

Here is a very strange looking bird. It has no wings. It has a very long bill, which it uses in gathering its food, which consists of snails, insects, and worms. It also uses its bill in another way. When resting it often places the tip of its bill on the ground, thus making the same use of its bill that an old man does of his cane when he leans upon it.

The archerfish has a special instrument. It is a sort of squirt gun for shooting insects. It not only can shoot them when they are still, but when they are flying. It watches the insect as it is flying over the water, and hits it with a fine stream of water shot from its mouth. The insect, stunned from the blow, falls into the water, and the fish eats it.

I could give you a great many more examples of the different tools that we find in animals, but these are sufficient. You can observe other examples yourself as you look at different animals.

# Review

1. For what does the sawfly use its saw?

2. What sort of useful work does the silkworm do for us?

3. Describe the special building functions of wasps and spiders.

4. What is the proboscis of an insect?

5. Describe the work of the tailor bird.

6. What special function does the archerfish have?

# Tools for Defense and Attack

Animals have various tools for defending themselves. Some have claws, some horns, some hoofs, some spurs and beaks, some powerful teeth, and some have stingers. They use these to defend themselves when attacked.

Man has none of these things. Why is this? It is because, as is with tools, he can invent instruments of defense, and with his hands he can use them. If men could not invent and use such weapons as spears, swords, and guns, they would stand a poor chance against some animals if obliged to contend with them. A lion or tiger could tear the stoutest man in pieces if the man had nothing but his hands to defend himself.

The fighting tools of some birds are very powerful. Here are a claw and a beak of a very cruel bird. How securely this claw could hold the victim, and how strongly this beak could tear it in pieces! They are very different from the slender claws and the light beak of such

birds as the canary. Here is a predatory bird, the eagle. It is perched on a rock, and has under its feet a lamb that it found in the valley below. The lamb had, perhaps, wandered from the flock, and as it was feeding, not thinking of danger, the eagle discovered it. Swiftly diving down, it caught the lamb with its strong claws and brought it up here. You see what a beak the eagle has to tear the lamb in pieces, that it may consume the meat.

The toucan, shown in this picture, has a larger bill than most other birds. It uses this tool for crushing and tearing its food, which consists of fruits, mice, and small birds. The edges of the bill are toothed somewhat like a saw, de-

signed to tear in pieces the little animals which this bird feeds on. But it can use its bill also for another purpose. It is a powerful instrument of defense for fighting off animals that attack it. The toucan makes its nest in the hole of a tree, which it digs out with its bill if it does not find one already made. There it sits, keeping off all intruders with its big beak. The mischievous monkeys are its worst enemies, but if they get a blow from that beak, they are very careful to keep out of the way of the bird afterwards. When the toucan sleeps, it manages to cover up this large bill with its feathers, and so it looks as if there is nothing but a great ball of feathers. There is one curious use that the toucan makes of its bill: it uses it to trim its tail, cutting its feathers as precisely as a pair of scissors would. It takes great care in doing this, evidently thinking that it is important to its appearance. It waits till its tail is full grown before it begins to trim it again.

The claws of the cat are used to hold rats and other rodents very tightly. If you see a cat do this, you will get some idea of the way in which a lion or tiger captures its prey. As your cat lies quietly purring in your lap, look at its paws. The claws are all concealed, and the paw, with its cushions, seems to be a very soft, gentle thing. But when you play with the cat using a ball of string, and as it tries to catch the string with its paw, the claws now thrust out like a powerful weapon, which it uses to catch rats and mice. There are muscles that work those claws when there is need of them. When the claws are not thrust out these muscles are relaxed, but they are ever ready to act when a message comes to them from the brain.

Did you ever wonder what the use is of those springy cushions in the cat's foot? They are to keep it from being jarred when it jumps down from a considerable height, as it often does. Other animals that jump also have them. There is another use for these cushions. They are of use to animals in catching their prey. If the cat had hard, horny feet as it went pattering around, the rats and mice would be alarmed and escape.

Some animals have horns, which they use in attack and defense, and very powerful weapons they can be. Animals that have horns often defend themselves successfully against the attacks of lions, tigers, and other predators with teeth and claws. Horned animals use their horns for goring. They can toss quite large animals up into the air with their horns. In this animal, called the koodoo, the horns are nearly three  feet long. You see that they have a beautiful spiral shape. Indeed, the whole animal is very handsome. It lives in South Africa in the woods at the side of rivers. You might suppose that it would be rather difficult to get around among the trees and bushes with such long horns, but the koodoo manages to do this very well by throwing its head back and letting its horns rest on its shoulders.

There are some animals that have very unique instruments of defense. The porcupine is one such animal. It is covered with two kinds of quills. One kind is long, slender, and curved. The others are short, straight, very stout, and have sharp points. Whenever the porcupine is chased by animals and finds that it cannot escape by running, it stops and bristles up all its quills, as you see in the picture here. It then backs up, so that the short, sharp quills

may stick into the animal that pursues it. Some people think the porcupine shoots quills at anyone that attacks it, but this is not so. However, if any of the quills happen to be a little loose, they may fall out or stick into the flesh of its adversary.

Here is a drawing of a swordfish. Its sword is made of bone, and is so strong that it has been known, on rare occasions, to pierce the bottoms of ships. In the British Museum there is a piece of ship hull with a broken sword pierced through it. The fish must have died very quickly, for the sword of the fish is necessary for its survival. This sword is a powerful weapon of defense or attack against other animals.

The sawfish has a saw instead of a sword. The teeth, you see, are on either side of the saw. This fish is very large, and uses its weapon with great effect when fighting with whales and other monsters of the deep.

The octopus has a curious way of escaping from attackers. It is a strangely shaped animal, as you see. It has eight long arms, covered with little suckers, which it uses to stick to rocks, or to tightly hold any fish or shell that it catches. The octopus has inside of it a bag filled with a dark inky fluid. It uses this as a means of defense in this way: if a larger fish chases it, it empties its ink bag in the water, and thus makes such a cloud that it blinds its pursuer. Then the octopus very easily escapes.

It has been many years since giant squids or cuttlefish were discovered. Before that, the largest known octopuses were thought to be about two feet in length. Victor Hugo, a French writer, described one that measured about three feet long. It was said to be native to the shores of France on the Mediterranean Sea. People thought this story had been made up, but the discovery of the much larger creatures proved the truth of the French tale.

Giant squids were discovered in the waters of the Grand Banks, near Nova Scotia, where many codfish are taken.

The body of the largest squid measured twenty feet in length. The two larger tentacles, or feelers, on this creature measured sixty feet more. The ink bags of these creatures are very large.

Whales without teeth feed on the soft animals of the sea, as they cannot crush those with bones, like fishes. Whales, therefore, eagerly chase the squids. We see how God has provided these soft and otherwise defenseless creatures with the means to confuse their enemies.

As with the octopus, the instant the squid senses danger, it shoot out its ink into the water, which makes a thick cloud so dark and so disagreeable that the enemy stops in terror, while the squid makes good its escape.

The stingray has two electrical batteries — that is, organs for making electricity—and it can give a shock when it pleases. If the fish is a large one, it can give a shock powerful enough to knock a man down. It can disable almost

any fish that attempts to attack it, and it probably uses its battery also to overcome its prey.

Here is an eel, called the electric eel, which has the same ability, and uses it for the same purposes. A sailor was once knocked down by the shock from one of these eels, and it was some time before he recovered his senses.

The different kinds of turtles, while they have no great means of attack, have a most extraordinary means of defense. They have a complete suit of thick, bony armor. Most turtles can draw in their heads and limbs out of sight. Some can shut up their armor as tight as a box, and so be secure against almost any attack. Here is a picture of the green turtle, which sometimes grows so large as to weigh as much as three or four men. It is found in the islands of the East and West Indies. Its meat is considered a great luxury. The beautiful tortoise shell, from which jewelry is sometimes made, is obtained from the armor of some kinds of turtles. The green and loggerhead turtles are very abundant on the coast of Florida. In the summer, during moonlit nights, they go ashore on the islands

to lay their eggs. The female turtle will creep slowly up above the high water mark, and then dig, with her hind feet, a deep hole; here she deposits her eggs, several hundred in number, at one time. She is so intent to finish her work that one may sit on her back until she has completed her task. The hole is then covered by sweeping the sand back, using hind legs. The eggs are good for food, and the meat of the turtle is also good.

The largest known turtle is the black leatherback, now seen frequently in the ocean off the Atlantic coast. It can grow to a length of nine feet.

# Review

1. What fighting instruments do birds have?

2. Describe how an eagle captures its prey.

3. What sort of weapon does the cat have?

4. Describe the swordfish and sawfish.

5. Describe the attack and defense tools of the octopus and the squid. How are they alike? How are they different?

6. What creatures feed on squids?

7. What tool of defense does the sea turtle have?

# Wings

Birds walk upon two legs, but instead of arms, they have wings. The bones in a bird's wing are very much like the bones in our arms and hands, but they are designed to make a framework for the feathers of the wing to spread out from.

A bird's wing, when it is stretched out, is very large. It needs to be large to do its work well. A bird could not fly with small wings. You know that even when you try very hard you jump up into the air only a very little way. But the bird goes up very easily, as high as it pleases, and does not seem to be tired. This is because its wings spread out so broadly, and its feathers catch the air, lifting it upwards.

This is the reason that birds need such large wings. As the bird rises by pressing upon the air, it must press on a good deal of air to do this. If it pressed upon only a little air it could not rise at all, because the air moves out of the way quickly when it is pressed down. Swimming is like flying in the water. As when water is pressed it does not move out of the way as easily as air does, the tail and fins of fish do not need to be as large as the wings of birds. For the same reason, hands and feet work well enough for us to swim with, though we cannot fly with them.

Here is a very large bird, the condor. Lifting such a heavy

body into the air requires very large wings, and you can see that it has them.

To work such broad wings, the bird has very stout muscles. You know how the breast of a bird stands out. You see it here in the condor. This is because the muscles with which it works its wings are there. You can see these muscles when a bird is cooked. The meat is very thick on the breastbone; thicker than in any other part of the body. If we had such large muscles on our breastbones we would look very strange. But we do not need such large muscles to work our arms as birds need to work their wings.

A man could not fly even if he had wings fixed onto his arms. It has been tried. I knew a man once who made wings for himself. After he had made them, he went up onto the roof of a shed to try them. He jumped off and flapped his wings, but down he came as if he had no wings, and he was so bruised that he had no desire to try the experiment again. Now why could he not fly? It was not because he lacked wings. There the wings were, and he had made them well, for he had shaped them like the wings of birds. They were large enough and light enough. The difficulty was that the muscles of his arms were not strong enough to work them well. They were designed for lifting, not flying. A man cannot be like a bird merely by having wings. He must have a bird's flying muscles, or he cannot fly.

Different birds have wings of different sizes. Those that fly very far and swiftly have the largest wings. The wings of the hen are not large enough to carry it far up into the air. The most that it can do is to fly over a very high fence. If its wings are partly clipped, or cropped, it cannot even do that. There are some birds that do not use their wings for flying. The ostrich, shown here, is a great runner. It cannot fly, but its wings help it run.

Most birds, however, have wings with just the right shape and strength to permit them to fly through the air.

How beautiful are the motions of birds as they fly in the air! How easily and gracefully their wings work! Watch

the bird as it flies up and up, and watch as it makes a turn, and comes down so swiftly on its outstretched wings, sweeping up at a distance. Then up it goes again before it finally comes down. The swallow, as it wings its way through the air, is, at the same time, searching for food. As it skims along close to the ground or the water, it catches any fly that happens to be in its way.

Especially beautiful are the motions of the hummingbird. See it as it stops before a flower, fluttering on its wings, or as it darts with them from one flower to another. The muscles of its wings are very nimble. Our muscles cannot make motions as quick as these.

Did you ever examine a feather from a bird's wing to see how curiously it is made? The quill part is very strong, but, at the same time, light. The plume is quite strong also. It is made up of many very thin and delicate flat leaves, as we may call them, which are locked together by fine ridges on their edges. If you separate them they flick back together and are locked as closely as before. You can see the ridges with a microscope or magnifying glass.

The bat can fly swiftly with the broad, light wings that it has. Did you ever observe how a bat's wing is made? It is a very curious and beautiful thing. It is constructed of a fine, thin skin, on a framework of long, slender bones. These are pieced together like the metal ribs of an umbrella; and the wings fold up somewhat like an umbrella. This is done whenever the bat is not flying. When it is on the ground it is very awkward in its movements. It cannot get a start to fly, so it pushes itself along with its hind feet, at the same time pulling at the ground by the hooks in its wings, first one and then the other. It never likes to be on the ground, so it roosts by hanging itself upside down and wrapping its body with its wings.

Here is a picture of the vampire bat, from South America. It lives by drinking the blood of animals as they sleep.

Nothing is more delicate than the wings of insects. They are like gauze, but they have a framework that makes them quite firm, similar to leaves, which have  veins to make them firm. Here is a drawing of the wing of a locust. But you cannot appreciate the beauty of insects' wings from such drawings. You must examine the wings themselves. Even the wing of a common fly is very beautiful, so delicate is its structure.

The wing of a katydid is peculiarly beautiful. You see that it is very delicate. It has a light green color. There is a rather thick, three-cornered ridge at  the wing where it joins the body. There is a similar ridge on its other wing as well. In the space within this ridge there is a thin but strong membrane or skin, so that it makes a kind of drumhead. It is the rubbing together of these two drumheads on the wings that makes the noise. It is a strange sound. It is not exactly music, but the katydids seem to enjoy making it.

The katydid commonly makes three rubs at a time with its wings. It sounds somewhat as if it said "katy-did," and its name comes from this. Sometimes there are only two rubs, and then you can pretend that it says "She-did" or "She-didn't." The katydids are quiet in the daytime, but when evening comes they are very noisy. It is often amusing to hear them as they begin just at dusk. One will begin, and perhaps say its "katy-did" several times. Then another on a neighboring tree will reply. After a little time the whole colony will be at work. Each one appears to rest after each rubbing, and so it seems as if they answered each other from one tree to another. It is curious that you can stop the noise of this insect at once by striking the trunk of the tree in which it is perched.

# Review

1. How are the bones on a bird's wings especially designed?

2. What special features enable the bird to fly?

3. Why can't man fly, even if he makes wings for himself?

4. Which bird has the largest wings?

5. Describe the various ways that birds use their wings.

6. Describe the structure of the feather.

7. Compare the wings of a bat to the wings of a bird.

8. Describe the wings of insects. What might some insects use them for, other than flying?

---

# Coverings for the Body

The skin of man is his covering. It covers up the body like a case. It keeps our bodies from being injured. How strange we would look if there were no skin to cover up these parts from view.

The skin fits all parts of the body very nicely. On the

hand it is like a glove. See how well it fits. But observe that there are some places where it is quite loose and full of wrinkles. It is like this between the thumb and forefinger, and around the joints of the fingers. In these places it would not do well to have a tight fit, because if it were tight you could not move your thumb and fingers as freely as you do.

The covering of man's body is different from those of the animals. It is, for the most part, bare skin, while most animals have hair, feathers, scales, shells, or hard plates like armor. Why is it that man's covering protects him so much less than those of animals? It is because he knows how to make coverings to put on over his skin. He can make coverings suited to the degree of heat or cold. But animals know nothing about this. No one ever saw an animal make clothes and put them on. The Creator has already given to each animal the covering it needs. Let us look at this a little.

Animals in very cold climates need very warm coverings. They therefore have thick fur. But animals that live in warm countries have rather thin hair instead of fur. The elephant has very little hair, and it is only with the greatest care that it can be made to live through cold winters in captivity. The same is true of the monkey. If these animals had a good covering of fur on their skins, the cold would not affect them so much.

The hair of the horse is rather thin. It is quite different from fur. If the horse's master is kind, he is very careful to put a good blanket on it whenever the cold makes it necessary. If the horse had no blanket in the winter, it would become cold and get sick. The horse is not a native of cold countries, but of warm countries such as Arabia. There, horses run wild in large companies or herds.

You know how thick the fur is on a cat. You can see how fine it is and how thickly the hairs clump together if you blow on it so as to separate the hairs. With this warm coat the cat does not feel the cold much. You can often see it out of doors in cold weather, with its feet gathered up under its body to keep them warm. The monkey, with its thin hair, could not do so. It has to be kept in a warm place in the winter.

The covering of birds, though it is designed to keep them warm, is very light. If it were not so, they could not fly very well. Feathers are so light that when we wish to speak of anything as being very light, we might say that it is as light as a feather. The downy feathers on the breast of the bird are especially light. The feathers of the wings are different. They are made strong for the work of flying, and at the same time they are quite light.

Birds that live primarily in the water have an oil to coat their feathers. This keeps them from being soaked. For this reason a duck, when it comes out of the water, is almost as dry as before it went in. But if a hen should go into the water in the same way, it would be soaked to the skin. It was not made to go into the water and has neither the oily feathers nor the webbed feet that are given to the duck.

Why is it that fish have scales? It is because they need a smooth covering in order to glide along easily in the water.

A rough covering, or one that would soak in water, would be bad for them. The scales lap over one upon another, as you see here in the picture of the herring. They thus make quite a firm coat of mail, and do not hinder the bending motions of the fish. If the covering were in a single piece instead of being made up of many scales, it could not bend as easily as it does now in turning its course in the water. The scales are kept smooth, and this helps the fish to glide along swiftly. It is this that makes the fish so slippery that it is difficult to hold as it struggles when it is taken out of the water.

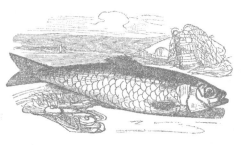

You have learned about the coverings of such animals as lobsters and crabs. There is one kind of crab called the hermit crab that has no covering over its tail as it has over the other parts of its body. It is therefore very liable to be injured unless it is guarded in some way. And how do you think the crab guards its tail? It just puts it into some shell that it finds, as you see here, and then goes about dragging it about wherever it goes. As the hermit crab grows, the tail becomes too large for the shell. So as soon as it feels the shell is too tight, it pulls its tail out and goes in search of another shell. It is amusing to see the crab try on one after

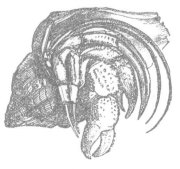

another until it finds one that fits well. Sometimes two of these crabs come to the same shell and fight over it.

The hermit crabs are subjects for our curiosity; for we wonder why they are not provided with hard shells for protection, which would seem to be better than depending upon the shells of other creatures. But we know from our faith in our great Creator that some wise purpose is served in such oddities. The hermit crab actually becomes better protected when it chooses the hard, cast-off shells of shellfish. They can draw themselves in and protect all tender parts from harm, keeping the stout claws uncovered for defense. The soft body of a hermit crab quite naturally winds up into the coil of a cast-off shell, and it seems as if the shell always belonged to it.

The great horse conch shell, as large as a man's head, is often found occupied by a large sea hermit crab. The long, soft body coils around the whorl inside and after some time it conforms itself to the shape of the shell, so that one would think it was made there. This heavy shell is carried wherever the hermit goes.

There are many small hermits, occupying the little turret shells that are commonly found on the seashore beaches, but there are some that live exclusively on land. One type of hermit crab that occupies a shell about the size of an apple and has pretty, red rounded claws, can be seen at Key West and Tortugas, on the Florida Reef. Its habits are much like those of burrowing insects. Many have been tamed and kept in confinement, and will eat from your hand. One was once found stuck to an old pipe bowl, instead of a shell. This shows the instinct of the creature to thrust its soft body into something for protection. Though this creature's body must have clung with difficulty to the inside of the pipe, it executed some feats quite remarkably. It frequently climbed up the corner of a set of drawers to drink from a saucer and was quite tame.

# Review

1. Describe the covering for man's body.

2. Where does it have wrinkles, and why?

3. How is the covering of man different from the coverings of animals?

4. Describe the various coverings of the elephant, monkey, cat, and horse.

5. Describe the coverings of birds and fish.

6. How is the hermit crab different from all other animals?

---

# Beautiful Animal Coverings

There is great variety in the coverings of insects. In some, the covering is like burnished armor. The variety of colors in these coverings is exceedingly great, many having a splendid brilliance. Some of the smallest insects that most people never notice are surpassingly beautiful when examined with the microscope. They are much like the smallest of flowers in this respect. We know not how much beauty there is all around us in the small things that God has created until we take the microscope and look at them.

The butterflies are among the most beautiful of insects. Almost every variety of color can be seen in them, and many colors are often seen together, arranged in the most beautiful manner. You may not have any idea of the great variety of their beauty until you see an encased collection of them at the museum.

Perhaps you have often admired the beauty of different seashells. These are the coverings of animals that lead a very quiet life, as you have learned about the oyster. The colors on the inside of these shells are often very splendid. Sometimes the outside of the shell is just as beautiful. But even if the outside is not at all handsome when we find the shell in the water, we often find that clearing off the outer coating with acid, or by rubbing, will reveal beautiful colors. By grinding the shell at different angles, layers can be seen shining with various hues.

The beauty of these coverings is of no use to the animals that live in them. They have no eyes to see it. So for what is it intended? It is for our enjoyment. The Creator scatters beautiful things even on the bottom of the ocean for us. If the shells of all animals that live there were as plain as that of the oyster, they would be just as useful and comfortable for them as are the ones they have decked with their elegant colors. As far as they are concerned, the beauty is wasted. But men gather the shells, and while they admire them, they can see the beauty that the Creator lavishes even in the depths of the sea as the evidence of His abounding goodness.

The beauty in the coverings of birds is just as great. The various colors in their plumage are arranged in every variety, and there are all shades of colors, from the most brilliant yellow to the richest black.

The greatest display of the plumage in birds is often in the delicate and downy feathers of their breasts. But in the bird that you see here, the hoopoe, its chief beauty is in its crest, which is orange tipped with black. It is one of the most elegant birds.

In the peacock there is a great display of colors. The animal struts about, and lifting its tail into the air, spreads it like a fan. It seems very foolishly proud of its beauty. Vain people generally have something disagreeable about them, and so it is with the peacock. Its voice is so harsh and screeching that no one would want it in their neighborhood.

Birds of paradise are exceedingly beautiful. There are several kinds of them. The most common kind is the one pictured here. I will give you an idea of its colors. Most of its body is a rich brown, the throat is a golden green, the head is yellow, and the long, downy feathers around the tail are a soft yellow. This elegant bird is very careful to prevent the smallest speck of dirt from getting on its plumage, and when it sits on a branch of a tree it always faces the wind so that its feathers will not be ruffled.

There may be in the hummingbirds more variety of color than in any other kind of bird. Their colors are very brilliant, especially in the delicate feathers of their breasts, and they are shaded in the most beautiful manner. There is hardly a finer display of colors than in a collection of hummingbirds at the museum. Here is an engraving of a few varieties of these birds. You can see what different shapes they have. They are alike only in their long, slender bills. When you see a large collection of them, with all their varied forms and colors, you will be filled with admiration and wonder.

Many animal furs have much beauty, but there is not as great a variety of color in animal furs as there is in the plumage of birds. As you blow on fine fur, and see how thickly its delicate fibers stand together, you cannot help but admire its richness. Each fiber is in itself a beautiful thing.

It is hard to understand why some animals that we dislike so much should have so much beauty. Worms and caterpillars may be disgusting to us, yet many of them have a great display of elegant colors. In the early summer you may see a caterpillar crawling along on the windowsill with its numerous feet of curious shape. Its color is a brilliant green. On its back three beautiful light yellow tufts stand up in a row. Behind these, on a dark stripe, are two fleshy-looking round bunches, which are a most brilliant red. On its side white hairs bristle out in bundles. Its head is red, and from it extend forward, in two bundles, dark colored, but very delicate, feelers. They are shaped like the feelers of the butterfly.

Why is it that so much beauty is given to such animals? It does not seem to be of any use. But this cannot be so, for God has a use for everything that He makes. We are to remember that He can make a thing beautiful as easily as He can make it plain. And it is just this lesson, perhaps, that he means to teach us when he clothes such creatures as worms and caterpillars in coverings of beautiful colors. It is different with us. We try to make beautiful only those things that we prize much. There are some things that would be a foolish waste of time for us to decorate. This is because we can do but little in making things beautiful. But there is no end to God's power in the creation of beauty. He can, by the word of His power, make just as many beautiful things as He pleases.

# Review

1. Describe the coverings of various insects.

2. Describe the variety in seashells.

3. Describe the peacock and the bird of paradise.

4. In what way is beauty found even in worms and caterpillars?

5. What purposes do the beauty and variety in animals serve?

# A Time for Sleep

All animals have their times for sleeping. It would not do for them to use the machinery of their bodies all the time. If they did, their bodies would soon wear out. The brain, nerves, muscles, and bones are all repaired during sleep, so that they may be ready for use again.

When you feel tired, it is because you have overworked the machinery of your body by using it. When you lie down and sleep, the muscles relax. Few messages pass through the nerves, and the brain is more or less at rest. But all this time that you sleep your blood keeps circulating, and the breathing goes on. Why is this? It is so that the repairing of your machinery may be done, so as to prepare the body for future work and play. The repairing is all done by your blood. Your blood is the material for repairing as well as for building, and it must therefore be circulating while you are asleep. Breathing must also go on to keep the blood in good order.

The body is constantly repairing itself even while you are awake. But it repairs itself faster when the machinery of the body is not in use.

The same is true of building the body. More building is done when you are asleep than when you are awake. You are growing all the time, but you grow most when you are asleep. And it is because the child is growing that he needs more sleep than the adult does. The baby is growing very fast, and so he sleeps a great deal of time in the day as well as in the night.

The night is given to us as the time for sleep. It is dark

and still then, and we can go to sleep easily. Most animals sleep through the night. The flies, bees, bugs, and birds have gone to rest to repair for the next day. So have the larger animals. But it is curious that some animals are busy in the night and take their sleep in the day. It is so with the owl and the bat. The katydid, you remember, does not begin its noise until evening.

People that stay up late at night and do not get up early in the morning make a great mistake. They do not use the right time for sleeping. They ought not to turn night into day, as bats, owls, and katydids do, for they are not made for it.

When you are tired and need sleep, the weariness is not merely in your muscles. If it were, then simply keeping still, without sleeping, would be enough to repair. But the brain and nerves need repairing as well as the muscles. As long as you are seeing, hearing, and feeling, the nerves are kept too busy to be repaired well, and as long as your mind keeps thinking, the brain cannot be thoroughly repaired. So, then, merely keeping still will repair only the muscles, and sleep is needed to repair the brain and the nerves.

You may have noticed that when you dream very much you are not as refreshed as when you sleep soundly. Why is that? It is because when you dream, the mind is not wholly at rest; the brain is working, so it is not thoroughly repaired.

Some animals sleep in another way as well. It is a very long kind of sleep known as hibernation, which lasts all winter. A great number of animals such as frogs, bats, and ground squirrels go into hiding places in the fall to sleep until spring comes.

This is a deeper sleep than the every-night sort, which many animals have during the winter. It is a different kind of sleep, called hibernation. In the sleep at night the blood keeps moving, and the animal breathes, but in hibernation there is only occasional breathing, and the blood almost stops circulating. All is as still as death. But there is life, as there is life in the seed, and in the trees that look so dead in the winter. It is life asleep. The warmth of spring wakes up the life in these animals, as it does the life in the trees. The blood then begins to circulate in them, and they come out from their hiding places.

You have learned that the sleep that some animals go into lasts through the winter. It may be made to last longer than this. Some frogs were once kept in this winter sleep for over three years in an icehouse, and then, on being brought out into the warm air, revived and hopped about as lively as ever. We do not know how much longer they might have been kept in this sleep. You perhaps remember about some seeds in which the life was asleep many hundreds of years. It may be that life might be kept asleep in frogs and other animals just as long by steady cold. A toad was once found in the middle of a tree fast asleep. How it came there was not known, but the wood had gone on growing year after year, and as there were sixty-seven rings outside of the toad, it was clear that it had been there sixty-seven years. A long sleep it was, but the toad soon woke up and hopped about, as alive as ever.

Yet, there are some animals that do not sleep wholly throughout the winter. The blood moves a little when it is cold, but when the weather is quite warm, they wake up just enough to eat a little. Now it is curious that such animals always lay up something to eat right alongside of them when they go into their winter sleeping places. But those that do not wake up at all usually do not lay up any food, for it would not be of any use. They are governed by instinct in this matter.

The field mouse lays up at its side nuts and grain, when it goes into its winter quarters, and when it is partially awakened by a warm day, it eats a little of its store. The bat does not lay up anything, although it wakes up when it is warm. It does not need to lay up anything, because the warmth that awakens it also wakes up gnats and insects on which it lives. It catches some of these, and then, as it finds itself going to sleep again, hangs itself upside down as before. The marmot or woodchuck does not wake up at all, but always lays up some dried grass in its hole. What is this for? The marmot feeds on it when it first wakes up to get a little strength before it comes out from its hole in the spring.

How much life, then, is asleep in the winter, in animals as well as in plants! And how busy life is in its waking in the spring! While the roots and seeds in the ground send up their shoots, and the sap again circulates in the trees and shrubs, and the buds swell, multitudes of animals are crawling out of their winter hiding places into the warm, balmy air. When the leaves are fully out, and the flowers abound, the earth swarms with busy insects and creeping things, of which we saw none during the winter.

Some of the birds that we see in the spring have not been asleep during the cold weather but have spent their winter in the South, and have now winged their way back to spend their summer with us. They go back and forth in this way every year, guided by that wonderful thing called instinct. How this makes them take their flight at the right time, and in the right direction, we do not understand. Only God knows exactly how and why His creatures act the way they do.

# Review

1. Why do animals sleep?

2. Why do you feel tired after work or play?

3. Why does the blood circulation and breathing continue when you sleep?

4. What happens to your body when you sleep?

5. Name some animals that sleep in the day and are active at night.

6. Why must one sleep instead of merely keeping the body still?

7. Describe the winter sleep of animals.

8. Do all animals hibernate? If not, then name some that do not.

# Chapter Seven

# The Crown of Creation

## The Superiority of Man

You have learned in earlier chapters about the human body as well as the bodies and functions of various animals. The physical make-up of animals is, especially with mammals, often similar to that of man. This is because both man and animals have a common Creator. The same God who designed and created your body also designed and created the forms and functions of all His creatures and instilled in them the marks of His creation.

It is because of the similarities in form and function between man and animals that many scientists falsely assume that man is only another kind of animal. Because of their unbelief in the God who created them, they use many confused methods of study and observation to conclude that man and animals descended from a common root. Man, they insist, descended from an ape-like animal with as little intelligence as the monkeys we see in the zoo to-day.

But it is impossible for them to prove such an idea, even with the billions of dollars that are being spent on such research, for it is impossible to prove a lie. The more bones that scientists dig out of the ground, looking for proof of their theory, the more they dig up the truth concerning the wonder of God's creation.

We know from the Creator's own Word that He created man different from animals. Unlike animals, man was created in the image of God, that is, in the likeness of the Creator Himself. Therefore there is a fundamental difference between man and animals. Man is unique. God formed man from the dust of the earth with His own hand and breathed life into him, thus giving him soul and mind as well as a body. In other words, unlike animals, man is created in two basic parts: the physical and the spiritual. Like animals, man's physical body was made from the elements that God had placed in earth, but he did not become a living being, or soul, until God breathed into him the breath of life.

By breathing into man the breath of life, God imparted to man many of His own attributes, or characteristics. This is the reason why man is able to discern both good and evil, and is given responsibility to do what is right before God.

Man is also given the gift of emotions and the ability to express them. The animals know nothing of wisdom, love, hatred, joy or sorrow. This power of knowledge and emotion is sometimes called the heart of man. This is not the physical muscle in your chest, which you have already learned of, for our minds and wills are also called our hearts. The animals are given no such discernment and no such heart, and therefore have no such responsibility before God.

The Bible tells us that men look at the outward appearance, but God looks at the heart. When people try to compare animals with man, they may be tempted to think that animals display the same feelings that people do, but they fail to consider that animals are not created with minds and hearts as men are.

Certain animals may seem to express some emotions, but this is because of the animal instinct that God has given them. God has created them with a predetermined kind of behavior. The beaver that seems to show intelligence in building his dam and his thatched house has been created especially for that purpose. It cannot possibly learn any other method of building or any other kind of behavior. The wasp that makes paper for its house does not do so because of any sort of learning or reasoning. It was created from the beginning with this behavior. Likewise with the spider weaving its web or the bird building its nest.

There is a story of a man who caught a young beaver and put it in a cage. After a while he let it into his living room where there were a great variety of things. As soon as the beaver was free from its cage it began to exercise its building instinct. It gathered together whatever it could find—brushes, baskets, boots, clothes, sticks, and bits of coal—and arranged them as if to build a dam. The beaver had no discernment of the fact that there was no water nearby and a dam would have been quite useless. All it could do was exercise the building instinct that had been given to it by the Creator.

The mother hen that watches over its eggs so carefully was designed to do so from the beginning of creation. If you put a duck's eggs in her nest she will sit on them as if they were her own eggs, and after the ducks are hatched she will care for them, not knowing that they are not chickens. It is amusing to see her when the ducks grow large enough to go into the water. Off they run, plunging into the water to swim about, while the hen stands by the water, greatly alarmed lest they should be drowned. She can have no understanding of the situation because she is acting only upon her instinct to protect her young, just as the ducklings are acting on their instinct to swim. If you place smooth round stones in the nest of a hen she will sit on them as if they were eggs. It is her instinct that makes her sit, regardless of circumstance and without any discernment.

Each generation of hens will do exactly as the one before it without any thought and without any learning. They do not need to be taught what to do. God has given them an instinct to survive and to safeguard the continued existence of their own species. The care of the hen, in

anything more than appearance, can in no way compare to the real love that a mother feels for her child.

Man is not given an instinct. Instead, God intends that we should exercise our minds to deliberately learn of His creation and to be trained to labor according to His will. Because God has given us minds and hearts to think and feel, we are responsible not only for our outward actions, but for our hearts as well.

Another aspect of man's nature makes him unique in all creation, for when a human being dies, his soul continues to live on, even when his body returns to the dust until the end of time. When God comes to judge the world at the end of history, the souls of people who have already died will be reunited with their resurrected bodies. On the Judgment Day, God will examine the heart of each person and will determine which actions or thoughts during their lifetime were good or evil. Since God requires human beings to be perfectly sinless, the only souls who will not be condemned on the Judgment Day are those whose sins have been covered by the perfect sacrifice of Jesus Christ on the Cross of Calvary.

Man is called the crown of God's creation. This is because man was intended by God to be the king of His creation. We are commanded to take dominion over—to rule—God's creation, which He has entrusted to us. We are to be managers of God's earth.

Dominion over other creatures is an important part of this command. So when a man keeps animals in captivity to tame them or use them for work or food, he is carrying out a part of his God given duty. Whether we use horses for riding, cows for obtaining milk, donkeys for plowing soil, or cattle for meat, we are seeking to fulfill the command that God has given to us. When people have cats or dogs as pets, taming them and keeping them for enjoyment, they are carrying out an aspect of God's creation mandate. It is the same when people catch fish and hunt animals for food and management. All these activities of man are included in God's command to take good care of His creation and to enjoy it. And God will hold men responsible for how they have fulfilled this command. (2 Corinthians 5)

Though man is created in the image of God, he has fallen from this original condition and become sinful. As a fallen creature, he is unable to fulfill God's righteous demands, which are expressed in His commandments. It is only when God grants to a person the gift of faith to trust in the grace and power of Christ as the Savior from sin, that such a one can fulfill the great Creation Mandate.

# Review

1. Why are some animals similar to man in form or function?

2. What falsehood do many people believe because of these similarities?

3. What is the fundamental difference between man and animals?

4. How did God create man?

5. What do animals have in the place of emotion and reason?

6. What great responsibility has God given to man concerning the earth?

7. What are some of the things that we do to obey this command?

# Hygiene and Diet

In some of the chapters you have learned how our bodies are made, and how they are kept alive. You have seen how much like machinery the different parts of the body are. God, our Creator, expects all people to take good care of the different parts of their bodies. It is important for us to do so, because we suffer if we do not. But it is also wicked if we neglect such duties, for God has given us life and the faculties for its preservation to a good old age. The knowledge and care that we use in such duties is called hygiene.

We do wrong if we do not carefully preserve our natural good health by the use of the faculties we have. One of the first and the simplest rules of health, or hygiene, we should heed is: be cleanly. No respectable person will long to be otherwise.

In your studies concerning the human body you find that the skin is full of pores that reach down to glands or little sacs. These give out a fluid we call perspiration. If one is not kept clean by frequent washing, the little pores often become filled up, the moisture hardens, and the free circulation is stopped. This is liable to harm your health.

Hygiene teaches us to learn of all we can about our bodies, and to use it always for the preservation of our health. It is very necessary to keep our hands and faces clean and dry, as many very dangerous diseases come right from carelessness in this matter. The feet should always be kept warm, and the shoes and stockings kept dry. Sitting in a draft of air in trains, cars, and other places, often causes serious illness because harmful germs from people sitting near you can travel through the air that you breathe. We should dress to preserve a uniform, comfortable condition, indoors or out. We should avoid being chilled, but if so exposed, we should get warm as soon as possible. Special care should be taken to warm the feet well after such exposure.

Hygiene teaches us to preserve health by eating and drinking what is known to be wholesome for us. Our parents are good teachers in such things. They usually give what is the best and advise against what is wrong and hurtful. Therefore it is wise and biblical for the young to observe, carefully and strictly, the advice of their parents.

It would seem that when you are old enough to notice the disgusting looks of a drunkard, and see the dreadful sufferings he brings on his family, his wife, and his children — their loss of home, and sufferings from starvation — all this, one would think, should caution us about the misuse of intoxicating drinks. Horrible beyond measure is the result to the drunkard, if he continues.

Drinking too much alcohol makes one want more, and it carries one onward to a bad end. One very bad result to excessive drinkers is the loss of moral faculty. Desire for drink overcomes them, and there is little to hold them from doing much that is evil. Such are easily led astray. This is a sad thing to reflect on, but it is very true. The Word of God warns people about the dangers of strong drink and the results of not drinking wine or similar drinks in moderation. (Ephesians 5:18, 1 Timothy 5:23, and 1 Peter 4:3)

There are many other things such as drugs or narcotics, which are such deadly poisons that one would think it unnecessary to caution people against their use. Do not dare to use any without your doctor's advice, for they are dangerous. They soon beget an appetite, called addiction, which brings ruin in every form. The stomach is disturbed, and many ailments are produced that you would shudder to know about.

Tobacco is another very useless substance that we should avoid. Smoking and chewing tobacco are harmful habits, and should be avoided. One would suppose that the nauseating effects of an experiment of smoking or chewing would prevent children from further attempts, but it seems grown-up, they think. Oh, no, it is not grown-up. Leave them alone. There are many reasons that smoking and chewing are very undesirable, besides being a danger to your health. Comfortable homes are quickly polluted by stale tobacco smoke. Even the floors are not free from the vile odor. No household where tobacco is used can be sweet and clean.

Perhaps the most common health problem facing many young people today is the lack of a proper diet and healthy exercise. Too many children eat huge quantities of fatty foods and frequently drink sugar-filled soda pop. The Bible commands all human beings to do all things in moderation and to avoid the sin of gluttony or over-eating. Great harm can come to youngsters who fail to exercise regularly and to those who insist on eating large quantities of unhealthy food.

The great Creator, Jesus Christ, requires each one of us to be good stewards of the things He has given to us. Perhaps our most important physical possession is our body. We should take good care of our earthly temples, for God will hold us responsible for how well we take care of His gifts.

Remember, my young friends, that your bodies are the Lord's handiwork. Work hard, therefore, to keep them healthy for the glory of Jesus Christ.

# Review

1. What is hygiene?

2. Why should we take good care of our bodies?

3. Describe how the pores of the skin function.

4. What does the Bible say about the use of alcohol?

5. What are the dangers of smoking?

6. What is gluttony? Why should we avoid it?

# Words You Should Know

## A

**Absorb**—to take in or assimilate.

**Addiction**—to be mentally or physically enslaved to a habit or substance.

**Artery**—the blood vessel that carries blood from the heart to the body.

## B

**Barb**—the pointed part of an object that hooks back from a main point.

**Bile**—a bitter yellow or green liquid in the stomach that helps in digestion.

**Breastbone**—the bone in the front of the chest where the ribs meet.

## C

**Capillaries**—fine hairlike blood vessels between the arteries and the veins.

**Captivity**—to be enslaved or imprisoned.

**Circulate**—to move in a circle, passing from place to place, and ending at the starting point.

# D

**Digest**—the process of changing food into a form that is easily absorbed by the body.

**Diverse**—of various kinds or forms.

**Down**—The soft feathers on the bird's breast.

**Duct**—A tube or pipe through which fluid or air is passed.

# E

**Enamel**—the hard covering on the crown of the tooth.

**Exoskeleton**—a hard external covering found in many invertibrates such as insects and shellfish.

# F

**Faculty**—the ability to perform a certain action.

**Fins**—the paddle-like parts of the fish, used for steering and stopping in the water.

# G

**Gizzard**—the muscular pouch in the stomach of many birds, which grinds food during digestion.

**Gland**—an organ in the body designed to produce fluid.

# H, I, L

**Hibernate**—to spend the winter in a deep sleeping state.

**Iris**—the colored part of the eye.

**Liquor**—strong alcoholic drink.

# M

**Membrane**—a thin layer of tissue.

**Mortar**—a mixture of cement used to bond bricks together.

# N

**Narcotics**—any addictive drug that numbs the senses.

**Nauseating**—causing sickness of the stomach.

# P

**Patella**—the kneecap.

**Pendulum**—a heavy hanging object that swings back and forth.

**Perspiration**—sweat.

**Plumage**—a bird's entire covering of feathers.

**Pore**—a tiny opening in the skin.

**Predatory**—preying on other animals for food.

**Prehensile**—designed for grasping or holding.

**Proboscis**—the protruding mouth in some insects.

**Pupil**—the part of the eye through which light enters.

---

# S, T

**Saliva**—a liquid produced in the mouth that helps in digesting.

**Tendon**—a cord of dense tissue that connects the bone with the muscle.

**Tentacles**—the long flexible arms of the octopus and the squid.

**Thatched**—covered with straw or leaves.

**Tobacco**—the plant used for cigarettes and other drugs.

---

# V

**Veins**—the blood vessels that carry blood from the body to the heart.